AF531564

PERSONALITY AND CREATIVITY OF BLIND

PERSONALITY AND CREATIVITY OF BLIND

By

SANTOSH ARORA

ANMOL PUBLICATIONS PVT. LTD.

NEW DELHI - 110 002 (INDIA)

ANMOL PUBLICATIONS PVT. LTD.
4374/4B, Ansari Road, Daryaganj
New Delhi - 110 002
Ph.: 3261597, 3278000
www.anmolbooks.com

Personality and Creativity of Blind

First Edition, 2002

ISBN 81-261-1145-3

PRINTED IN INDIA

Published by J.L. Kumar for Anmol Publications Pvt. Ltd., New Delhi - 110 002 and Printed at Mehra Offset Press, Delhi.

CONTENTS

PREFACE

The National Policy of Education (1986) has made a significant contribution towards developing educational opportunities for handicapped children and their education has been recognised as a human resource development activity rather than a mere welfare activity. The centrally sponsored scheme of Integrated Education for Disabled Children (IED) is geared to realize this objective and is supported by the Committee for Review of National Policy of Education (1990).

Legally speaking the government and society should spend at least the proportionate amount meant for these exceptionals since constitutionally every individual has a right for his maintenance and education. If the exceptionals are ignored and the money from the public funds which is their share is spent on normal children or elsewhere, it is nothing short of robbing the under privileged and is unfair to these exceptional, who are unable to raise their voices and revolt or demand attention, as they are helpless.

Thus there is an immediate need for the improvement of special education to exceptionals who need special class rooms, special instructions, specially trained teachers, special curricula and good competencies, and make them independent, instead of liabilities to the society/nation. So, every handicaped individual should be imparted the appropriate education on humanitarian grounds. As Edwin W. Martin (1976) said, Special educators know that the promise of an appropriate education for every handicapped child or for each gifted child will not be fulfilled by the passage of a law or by enrolling each youngster in a programme.

Blind children face many difficulties in learning through printed language. These children are found to be handicapped to varying degrees in regard to educational achievement. Reading ability which relies heavily upon print language as well as perceptual skills and is probably the most important aspect of academic achievement gets seriously compromised. It can be very difficult for Blind children to understand and use abstract concepts when they are not familiar to their environment.

An indepth exploration of the personality of blind children and normal children will be helpful in developing and designing the essential educational infrastructure for them. Thus, besides aiding in formulation of the personality structure and development of creative abilities of visually impaired, it would be helpful in the development of the methodology for teaching as well as development of curriculum and an effective teaching learning environment. Creativity is a aspect of personality. Personality is an affective aspect and creativity is a congnitive aspect. These are interactive with each other in such individuals. In other words this is an attempt in which creativity has been studied as an integral component of personality functioning in interaction with the total personality. The first chapter deals with the problem and background. The theoretical aspects of personality and creativity have been outlined. Need and significance of the study has been discussed in this chapter.

In the second chapter, studies related with the present problem have been thoroughly reviewed. Personality and other psychological and behavioural aspects within studies have been explored as regards to type of blindness and gender differences. Studies on personality and creativity and other related studies have been surveyed on the basis of sex difference, type of blindness, blind and normal children.

The design and procedure of the study has been dealt with in the third chapter wherein the sample and tools used in the study have also been elaborated.

The results of the study regarding personality and creativity have been depicted in the tabular and graphical form in the fourth and fifth chapters. The sixth chapter deals with interpretation in the form of personality profile.

The findings of the study have been discussed in the seventh chapter wherein the findings related with personality and creativity have been elaborated.

The eighth chapter includes educational implications and remedial programme and new areas of future research have also been suggested in it.

The ninth chapter deals with the vocational opportunities for blind. Various governmental and non governmental organizations of vocational training programme have been outlined.

Very exhausted references have been quoted under bibliography.

The study was undertaken under the able guidance of Dr. K.C. Vashistha, Reader, Dayalbagh Educational Institute, Dayalbagh, Agra. His critical evaluation and worthy suggestions were immensely helpful.

I must express a deep sense of gratitude to Prof. Beena Shah, Director, IASE, MJP Rohilkhand University, Bareilly for their valuable comments.

My interactions with Prof. C.L. Kundu, Prof. S.C. Ghosh, Prof. P.C. Saxena, Prof. Lokesh Kaul, Prof. S.P. Ruhella, Prof. R.P. Srivastava and Prof. C.P.S. Chauhan helped me a great deal in clearing the mist. I am thankful to all of them.

I also owe my gratitude to my brother Mr. M.M. Arora for his constant encouragement and Co-operation in every phase of the study.

Finally, I am thankful to M/s Anmol Publications Pvt. Ltd., New Delhi for publishing this work.

—**Santosh Arora**

1

INTRODUCTION

Universally in the past, handicapped children were excluded from the purview of nominal experience. They have been treated as defective beings and believed that these children will not profit from regular schools and their facilities. The handicapped were viewed as the dregs in society or as bad men who were prevented their participation in the activities necessary for survival. In the early nineteenth century as the idea of democracy, individual freedom and egalitarian swept in the west and advances in learning theory and technology have contributed to the emergence of optimistic attitude towards these pupil. The most positive response to this section of the society was envisaged by UNESCO in the 1946. The Education for All Handicapped Children's Act *(U.S. Public Law, 94-142)*, the *Warnock Committee* 1978 review report on the educational provisions for the handicapped children and youth in England are milestones in the care and education of the handicapped. In Indian Educational Provisions for Handicapped Children have become a priority as a result of the National Policy on Education 1986. This policy possessed all the favourable ethos as it commenced, just before the *International year for Disabled Persons* 1987 and launched during the *World Decade of Disabled Persons* 1983-92 as declared by UN General Assembly. All these attempts brought the galore of publicity on the needs of the blind in the world and in India.

The needs for a comparative study of the blind and the

sighted subjects arises from the fact that in India alone one third of the world's blind population resides. India's share is about 8-9 million. Blindness has a definite and distinctive effect upon the development of the individual's personality, because at least 75 to 80 percent of all impressions which the sighted ones get are registered through the sense of sight. Thus, blindness is a severe handicap. There is little empirical research in this area. Research on development of their personality has so far been neglected due to the inadequate tests and measurement techniques.

Blindness from birth need not by itself cause serious developmental delays. Yet we know that a large number of congenitally blind children do meet with grave difficulties that result finally in deviant personalities. These children suffer in a number of ways of which affectionate deprivation becomes the most acute and all pervading. Affectional deprivation comprises of unsympathetic behaviour, less attention, insecurity and leads to neuroticism, anxiety, maladjustment, aggression and a host of other problems. A blind person in India lives under a curse. He or she is a burden on his family and is either abandoned or allowed to waste away. A report on blindness in India- 1944 referred as *The burden of blindness is not that you can not see the light, the people, houses and landscapes around you; it is that you have nothing to do to fill the long, endless weary hours of darkness, that you are condemned to poverty and misery, and that you can not take part in the social life around you. Modern welfare does away with all this. The blind person is really extraordinarily normal. Give them a normal upbringing, schooling, train them in a useful trade and provide conditions favourable to their work, they can become as useful a citizen as any others and of course, the happiest man on earth.*

The aim of the present study is to compare the personality factors and creative potential of blind and normal children in order to understand their personality vignette. This understanding will help the blind to develop better interpersonal and emotional relationships, thereby integrating them into the normal stream of the sighted world.

Moreover, creativity is one of the highly valued human qualities, which is exclusive to a systematic enquiry on blind children. Lowenfeld 1950 beautifully suggested that blindness limits cognition by restricting (i) range and variety of experiences, (ii) the ability to get about, (iii) control of environment and the self in relation to it. Villey 1930 echoed *No Mental faculty of the blind is affected in any way, and all of them, under favourable circumstances, are susceptible of blossoming out of the highest degree of development to which a normal being can aspire.*

1.1 A BRIEF HISTORICAL REVIEW

The history of special education has visualized many ups and downs in its progressive phases of development. It has been illustrated as-

(i) *Pre-Christian Era,* when disability was viewed as punishment for past sins and nobody wanted to interfere in the justice meted out the disabled persons by God;

(ii) *Christian Era-* when they were protected and pitied to reduce their pains and miseries.

(iii) *Dawn of 19th century-* when institutions were established to provide them separate education.

(iv) *Late 20th century-* when movement started to integrate them in the society;

(v) *Present age-* when the concept of special and integrated system of education has been involved on the basis of the needs of disabled persons.

In this context the most generous response to this section of the society was envisaged by UNESCO in the year 1946 Act. In keeping the NPE's objectives, the NCERT has formulated the *Project Integration for the Disabled* (PID) -1987 and stressed the need to strengthen the scheme of *Integrated Education for Disabled Children* (IEDC). It was brought out to help these children under the provision of *"Equal Educational*

TABLE 1.1 Population of Disabled by Age-Groups and Nature of Disability in 1981 (In Millions)

Disa-bility	*Age Group*										*Grand Total*
	0 - 4		5 - 14		15 - 19		60 +		Total		
	R	U	R	U	R	U	R	U	R	U	
	1	2	3	4	5	6	7	8	9	10	11
VH	2359	4554	92351	34268	693182	171500	2045183	355837	2856575	566159	7422734
HH			439368	96107	462450	244680	916857	202577	2818675	543364	3262039
SH			575096	168975	688381	199142	99431	24145	1362914	392262	1755176
LH	235077	98366	945900	282806	2094432	500714	913019	192302	4238428	1074138	5312616
	237436	102920	2052715	582156	4938445	1116036	3974490	774861	11276592	2575923	17752565

Source: Based on prevalent Data given in Nineteenth and Twenty-eighth of National Sample Survey Organisation and Total Population in the Population Statistics Paper-2 of 1983, A.G. office, Delhi (excluded Mentally Handicapped).

Opportunities". The objective of the policy is to integrate the handicapped with general community as equal partners, to prepare them for normal growth and to enable them to face life with courage and confidence.

Consequently, the *National Commission on Teachers* also stressed the need for recognizing special Education (MHRD, 1985). *The Programme of Action* (POA, 1986) envisaged expansion of educational provision for the disabled children to achieve the goal of universalization of primary education. *The Ram Murti Committee* 1990 however, emphatically suggested the general system of education to take care of the education of all children.

1.2. PREVALENCE IN INDIA

The data base on disabled persons is inadequate. The research efforts present divergent assessment of the blind population in India, while the National Sample Survey Organization (NSSO) gives the figure of just three and half million. The Indian Council of Medical Research concludes on the basis of its own survey that India has own fewer than nine million visually handicapped people. This also corroborate with the estimate provided by Vyas 1989 that the number of school age visually handicapped children in 1966 was four lakh. The table (1.1) speak itself for the highest rate of prevalence:

In a cynical way, it may be remarked that the population of visually handicapped persons in India equals the total population of several European countries. To compound the problem, visually handicapped children have seldom received adequate attention from public, press and legislature. This indifference to visually handicapped children is also reflected by scant research attention paid to them.

According to the *Revised POA, (1992)* about 12.59 million children with disabilities can be provided with education at the school stage. The details are given below:

	Types of Disabilities	*Figures in millions*
(i)	Locomotor handicapped	1.48
(ii)	Hearing handicapped	0.65
(iii)	Speech handicapped	0.91
(iv)	Visually handicapped	0.15
(v)	Mentally retarded	3.60
(vi)	Learning disabled	3.60
(vii)	Children with disability in the age groups of 16-18 years	2.20
	Total	12.59

The scenario is dismally dark especially as statistics show that the highly prevalent rate of visual impairment has attracted a meagre attention of the planners in order to the provisions made by them for their improvement and early intervention and ECCE Services (.15 million). They are still awaiting for the better treatment by the researchers at turn of the century.

More gloomy scenario has been presented by the Uttar Pradesh as it has higher rate of prevalence of blindness 1.54 % than the national rate (1.4%). To light this menace, the Central Government has allocated a large sum (Rs. 22.79 million) in 1993-94 to Uttar Pradesh (HT, Oct. 10,1993)

CAUSES OF VISUAL IMPAIRMENT

Blindness can be resulted due to many causes, each of which may have implications for development. It may be a consequence of environment factors that acted before, during or after birth, or it may be a genetic cause manifested as either a congenital and adventitious. Comprehensive classification of the causes of visual impairment is given here under:

I. Genetic Causes of Visual Impairment

(i) Mulifactorial Inheritance

(a) Buphthalmos

(b) Colobama & Myopia

(ii) Autosomal Recessive Inheritance

(a) Retinal aplasia

(b) Retinal degeneration with primary muscular involvement

(c) Albinism

(d) Others.

(iii) Autosomal Dominant Inheritance

(a) Retinoblastoma

(b) Congenital and infantile cataract

(c) Aniridia

(d) Others.

(iv) Chromosomes-linked Inheritance

(a) Pseadoglioma and congenital of infantile cataract

(b) Others, including choroideraemia.

II. Acquired Causes of Visual Impairment

(i) Prenatal e.g. cataract due to rubella

(ii) Postnatal e.g. opticatrophy due to meningitis

(iii) Perinatal e.g. retrolental fibroplasia.

PSYCHOLOGICAL AND BEHAVIOURAL CHARACTERISTICS OF BLIND CHILDREN

The blind, no doubt, are in minority in the world. They differin their characteristics, needs, accomplishments and behaviours from thoseof the sighted, ones thus assigning the sighted a dominant position in social situation.

The blind deal of speculation exists regarding the characteristics of the blind. Mental potentialities were presumed to be normal in this medical anomaly. Some believe that blindness is a handicap not only because it decreases mobility, but also it is accompanied by the lack of initiative and spontaneity. Mickell (1953) observed that the blind pre-school child has its own unique pattern of growth. It takes longer for him to progress in walking talking and also in motor coordination, as the typical eye-hand coordination in his case has been substituted by ear-hand coordination.

The blind children show many problems such as in behaviour in learning, in placement and social adjustment. Some children suffer from other sensory difficulties as well. The objects of learning are also sometimes too large or not easily accessible for them in order to enable them to touch, taste, smell, or listen to them.

Language and Speech Development

Language is the tool with which human being express themselves, and it is one of the most important factors in making human being superior to all other species. In the formal educational system language plays a very crucial role. Most of the children acquire language naturally without any formal training but severely blind children do not acquire language like others. As Northern and Down (1974) put it, *All the progress that man made, if one can call a highly technological society progress, is due sophistication in the manipulation of language . . . It follows that language deprivation is the most serious of all deprivations for it is used as a measure of our own humanness. Whether caused by sensory deprivation, to some degree, it keeps one from the complete fulfillment of one's power.*

Bericland (1952) summarizes observation of various authors of differences of speech in blind and seeing children as follows:

(i) The blind show less vocal variety.

(ii) Lack of modulation is more critical among the blind.

(iii) The blind tend to talk louder than the sighted.

(iv) The blind speak at a slower rate.

(v) Less effective use of gesture and bodily action is typical of the blind.

(vi) The blind use less lip movement in articulation of sounds.

Intellectual Abilities and Educational Achievement

Blind children have poor academic achievement even if they use large types of Braille. They are noted to be retarded by at least one or two year and are found to be under-achievers. Visual impairment is the main factor for slower acquisition of information by observation. Blind children have a slower reading rate and lack concreteness in instructional procedures.

Although blind pupils show grade by grade about the same achievement as seeing pupils. Hayes (1950) points out that: Blind children average at least two year older than seeing children in the same grades, so comparisons by age, either chronological or mental, demonstrate their retardation. Blind children are frequently handicapped by varying degree in educational achievement and reading ability both of which rely heavily on language skills.

Creativity

Creativity is one of the highly valued human quality which permits the individual child to express himself according to his mode of functioning. Creativity is an important means of adjustment. By realising emotional tension and rigidity it can help to overcome isolation from the environment and feeling of inferiority. Lowenfeld (1950) concluded that the blind are capable of achieving simultaneous spatial images through an act of integration of successively perceived factual impressions. He also concludes that in the modelling of the blind in modelling is a perspective of value. So far as creative activities of blind children are concerned, he warns of the danger of imposition of visual characteristics by the teacher and stress that the most primitive creative work born in the mind of a blind person and produced with his own hands is of greater value than the most effective imitation.

Personality

Personality and social development depend upon communication. Social interaction may be defined as the communication of ideas between two or more people. Many researches have found that visually impaired have different personalities and social characteristics compared to those of sighted children (Crandell, 1991, William, 1983). Behavioural problems depend upon the acceptance of the disability in the child's environment. As McAndrew (1948) reported that the deaf and the blind have smaller life- span than the normal, being partially isolated from the objective environment in which they live by the barrier qualities of their handicaps, and that they, therefore, develop less differentiated and more rigid personalities.

Blind children are looked down upon and ridiculed by normal children every now and then. They face both personal and social adjustment problems, because of this they feel inferior and ultimately this leads to maladjustment. Sommers (1944) has made an attempt to explore the answer to the problem of how to effect a more satisfactory development in the personality of handicapped children would seem to lie in building up in the parents of these children wholesome attitude towards the handicap, as well as in the education and guidance of the child himself.

Most of the researches reveal that blind children had a good level of home adjustment but emotional, social and educational adjustment of visually impaired children was poor than the sighted ones.

THE STATEMENT OF THE PROBLEM

Having now reviewed the various issues of blindness from different angles, it is clear that the field has vast developmental potential for psychological and educational explorations. However, it is yet an untouched and a virgin field of research under the domain of special education. Hence the researcher feels it worthwhile to study the personality and creative potential of blind children in greater detail specially in order to better identify those areas in their personality which are effectively manipulable as well as beneficial towards a more satisfying adaptation to the world. Thus the present problem can be stated as:

> A Comparative Study of the Personality and Creative Potential of Blind and Normal Children.

AIMS AND OBJECTIVES OF THE STUDY

The researcher has laid down the following objectives in order to explore the personality and creative potential of blind and normal children:

1. To identify the personality factors of blind and normal children.
2. To determine the creative potential of blind and normal children.
3. To compare the personality factors of congenitally and adventitiously blind children.
4. To measure the differences on creative potential of congenitally and adventitiously blind children.
5. To identify the gender discrimination among the blind and non impaired children in relation to personality factors and creative potential.
6. To draw the personality profiles of the above groups and suggest remedial programme for their education.

HYPOTHESES OF THE STUDY

The following null hypotheses have been formulated in the present study:

1. There exists no significant difference between the blind and normal children in relation to personality factors.
2. There exists no significant difference between the blind and normal children in relation to creative potential.

3. There exists no significant difference between the congenitally and adventitiously blind children in relation to personality factors.
4. There exists no significant difference between the congenitally and adventitiously blind children in relation to creative potential.

JUSTIFICATION OF THE STUDY

The most important element in the approach to the solution of the problems presented to schools and communities by these exceptional groups is recognition of the personality and creativity of the child and his various relationship with the family, community and general society and of the relative part to be played by clinics, schools, and other agencies of care, correction and education.

Each individual in a democracy has the fundamental right to physical up keep and education. In this context the report of the National Association of Secondary School Principals 1974 cites: *The same personal urges for affection, security and self-realization are paramount in all groups. Certainly, the social demands for vocational efficiency, intelligent citizenship, good character and all the values that constitute a suitable society are equally desirable for every type of individual, whatever the gifts and limitations.*

Society can never ignore the existence of these children or their problems; indeed, it has the responsibility of their custody, care, training and education. These children differ from normal in different aspects and require special education which may be conducted in separate classes in ordinary schools or in special institutions meant exclusively for these children.

Several studies conducted in foreign countries, reveal that blind children have many emotional maladjustment, intellectual, creative and behavioural problems (Crandel, 1978; Verret, 1992; Gilbertson, 1991; Lukoshe & Vichene, 1987). Due to lack of good perceptual skills, development is greatly affected, with lack of vision creating a barrier for normal communication. More personality problems are noticed in partially sighted children than in totally blind children. In America, Public Law 94 - 143, contains a mandatory provision, the Education for All Handicapped children Act, which states, In order to receive funds under the Act every school system in the nation must make provision for a free appropriate public education for every child between the ages of 3 and 21, regardless of how seriously he may be handicapped.

The National Policy of Education (1986) has made a significant contribution towards developing educational opportunities for handicapped children and their education has been recognised as a human resource development activity rather than a mere welfare activity. The centrally sponsored scheme of Integrated Education for Disabled Children (IED) is geared to realize this objective and is supported by the Committee for Review of National Policy of Education (1990).

Legally speaking the government and society should spend at least the proportionate amount meant for these exceptional since constitutionally every individual has a right for his maintenance and education. If the exceptional are ignored and the money from the public funds which is their share is spent on normal children or elsewhere, it is nothing short of robbing the under privileged and is unfair to these exceptional, who are unable to raise their voices and revolt or demand attention, as they are helpless.

Thus there is an immediate need for the improvement of special education to exceptional who need special class rooms, special instructions, specially trained teachers, special curricula and good educational programmes to develop their potentialities, confidence and competencies, and make them independent, instead of liabilities to the society/nation. So, every handicapped individual should be imparted the appropriate education on humanitarian grounds. As Edwin W. Martin (1976) said, Special educators know that the promise of an appropriate education for every handicapped child or for each gifted child will not be fulfilled by the passage of a law or by enrolling each youngster in a programme.

Blind children face many difficulties in learning through printed language. These children are found to be handicapped to varying degrees in regard to educational achievement. Reading ability which relies heavily upon print language as well as perceptual skills and is probably the most important aspect of academic achievement gets seriously compromised. It can be very difficult for blind children to understand and use of abstract concepts when they are not familiar to his environment.

Most educational systems use print and written language as the vehicle of learning. As a result, individuals with a vision loss, especially if it is severe or profound, are at a distinct disadvantage in the learning process. This is not because the education of blind has been consistently inadequate on the contrary, there has been much progress in the file. There is, however, a tendency to inappropriately judge the blind by the standard used to measure the achievement of normal peers.

An indepth exploration of the personality of blind children and normal children will be helpful in developing and designing the essential educational infrastructure for them. Thus, besides aiding in formulation of the personality structure and development of creative abilities of visually impaired, it would be helpful in the development of the methodology for teaching as well as development of curriculum and an effective teaching learning environment. Creativity is a aspect of personality. Personality is an affective aspect and creativity is a cognitive aspect are interactive with each other in such individuals. In other words this is an attempt in which creativity has been studied as an integral component of personality functioning in interaction with the total personality.

DELIMITATIONS OF THE STUDY

The present study has been delimited by the researcher in the following manner:

1. The study consisted of only Blind and non impaired children of both sexes.

2. The Blind sample of the study has been taken from the following special school.
   - (i) Ahmadi Blind School, A.M.U. Aligarh
   - (ii) Model School for Blind, NIVH, Dehradun.
   - (iii) Govt. Boys for Blind, NIVH, Delhi.
   - (iv) Rashtriya Virjan- Andh Kanya Vidhyalaya, New Delhi.
3. The study consisted only congenital and adventitious Blind children of both sexes.
4. The main tool of the study is 16 Personality Factory Questionnaire and Verbal Test of Creativity, while the other tools viz General Information Questionnaire, Socio-economic Status Scale are used only for the selection of the sample and for matching purpose.
5. The Sample consists of only 100 Blind and 100 normal of the age group of 13-18 years from the selected institution.

OPERATIONAL DEFINITIONS OF THE TERMS USED

Statement of the problem consists of many terms which required further definitions in relation to the present study. These terms are as following.

I. Personality

The world Personality has the most fascinating history and equally important to psychologists, educationists as well as for commoner. It is derived from *Latin world PERSONA and interestingly makes its way into French as (PERSONNALITIE & in German as (PERSONILICHKEIT) & into English as (PERSONALITY);* languages.

The first ever attempt has been made by Ordon W.Allport 1938, in his book Personality; A Psychological Interpretation to put forth a comparative definition of these psycho-physical systems that determine his unique adjustment to his environment.

In this study the world Personality has the following connotations: Personality is congregation of the 16 Factors of an individual which make him unique in his behaviour. These 16 personality factors are suggested by Cattell (1972).

Table 1.2: Details of 16 Personality Factors Developed by Dr. R.B. Cattell and Indigenously Adopted by Dr. S.D. Kapoor

S.NO.	*PF(Symbol)*	*Description of Personality Factor*
1.	A	Reserved Vs out-going
2.	B	Less Intelligent Vs More Intelligent
3.	C	Affected by felling Vs Emotionally stable
4.	E	Humble Vs Assertive
5.	F	Sober Vs Happy-go-lucky.
6.	G	Expedient Vs Conscientious
7.	H	Shy Vs Venturesome
8.	I	Tough- minded Vs Tender- minded.
9.	L	Trusting Vs Suspicious.
10.	M	Practical Vs Imaginative
11.	N	Forth right Vs Shrewd.
12.	O	Placid Vs Apprehensive
13.	Q1	Conservative Vs Experimenting.
14.	Q2	Group dependent Vs Self- sufficient
15.	Q3	Un-disciplined self- conflict Vs Controlled
16.	Q4	Relaxed Vs Tense.

II. Creative Potential

Creativity is a universal ability. It is present in same manner in everyone. Guilford's presidential address to the American Psychological Association was the first step of stimulating research in the field of creativity. According to Warren Creativity is the capacity of certain individuals to produce composition of any sort (works of art, mechanical devices etc.) which are essentially novel or which were previously unknown to the producer.

Guilford (1970) explains: that creativity is an ability to bring something new into existence. Guilford and Chirstensen (1956) have suggested that Fluency, Flexibility, Originality, Re-definition and Elaboration are the most important characteristics of creativity and it is believed that taken together they would give a reliable and valid information about the creative potential of the individual.

Since the researcher has selected the Baqer Mehdi verbal test of creativity, it is desirable to say few words here about these most important components of creativity. Verbal Test of Creativity consider that only three components of creativity viz. Fluency, Flexibility and Originality, brief description of these component as follows:

(a) Fluency

The ability to generate ready flow of ideas, possibilities, consequences and objects. This ability relates to production of ideas, alternative possibilities and objects in a particular situation.

(b) Flexibility

The ability to use many different approaches or strategies in solving a problem, the willingness to change direction and modify given information. This ability carries forward the process of production of ideas, it leads to the process of selection of appropriate possibilities from those available for a given situation and also modify it, if situation demands.

(c) Originality

The ability to produce clever, unique and unusual responses, the first two abilities increase the probability of producing unique and novel responses. It results in invention of new creations in music, dance, drama, painting sculpture and literature. If reflects the quality of the production envisaged in the first two abilities.

III. Blind Children

The American Medical Association proposed the definition of visually impairment in 1934, and it is now accepted by the American Foundation for the Blind,

A legally Visually impaired person is said to be one who has visually acuity of 20/200 or less in the better eye even with correction, or whose field of vision in narrowed so that the widest diameter of his visual field subtends an angular distance no great than 20 degrees.

Visual impairment have three conditions i.e., congenital visual impairment, adventitious impairment and partially sighted.

(a) Congenital Blind Children

A congenitally blind person is one who has never experienced sight and is unable to visualize visual concepts. Since a congenitally blind person has never seen, such a person has to conceptualize ideas about objects and reality through any means other than vision.

(b) Adventitious Blind Children

An adventitiously blind person is one who has developed blindness later in life. His loss of sight, which may be gradual or abrupt, has taken place after experiencing the world first through the medium of vision.

(c) Partially Sighted

Such a person does not lack total vision; a person with less than 20/200 vision after correction, is however, blind in legal term. The adaptation process of the partially visually handicapped is not the same as that of the completely blind.

In this study sample consists only congenital and adventitious Blind children.

OVERVIEW OF THE CHAPTER

This chapter provides an extract of the problems and conditions of the visually-impaired children. A sketch of the history of the efforts of the initiators has been drawn. The impediment to educational achievement and development of personality and creativity due to visual impairment have been reviewed. The prevalence of visually impairment in India has been seen as substantial and an effort made to signify efforts in the direction of the understanding and development of methods of teaching for Blind students.

2

CONSPECTUS OF THE LITERATURE

The personality of an individual is rooted in one's culture. In order to identify the culture and social factors that go into the development of personality, it become necessary to study and specifically to locate the determinants of the personality variables.

In this chapter the studies on blind and normal children have been split into (a) Foreign studies (b) Indian studies. The studies on visual impairment under each of these classes have been further divided into the following dimensions:

1. Achievement and Intelligence
2. Adjustment
3. Anxiety
4. Concept Formation
5. Creativity
6. Education
7. Emotional Development
8. Language Development
9. Personality
10. Value and Mannerism

A. FOREIGN STUDIES

(i) Achievement and Intelligence

Wan-Lin and Tait (1987) investigated the cognitive development of blind and sighted children through a Piagetian Conservation Scale. The sample consisted of 80 blind and 40 sighted children in the Republic of China. The result showed that vision contributed the important role in attainment of conservation in Blind subjects. The order of difficulty of conservation task for partially sighted subjects were more similar to sighted subjects than the blind children. Blind children differ from the sighted and partially sighted in relation to cognitive development.

Gutterman, Marjorie and Genshaft (1985) examined the correlation of Perkins- Binet Test of Intelligence Scale of the WISC-R and Wide Range Achievement Test (WRAT) which were administered on 52 low vision children. The results indicate that the mean scores on the two tests of intelligence were significantly different. The study suggested that Perkins-Binet Test of Intelligence Scale of the WISCR-R is not appropriate for use with low vision children because it is psychometrically inadequate and less reliable and valid.

(ii) Adjustment

Verret (1992) conducted a study to find out the community adjustment and vocational stability of Blind children. The sample consisted of 70 blind graduates. The community adjustment was assessed by Scholok's Community Adjustment Questionnaire and vocational stability was assessed by Hasazio's Questionnaire. The result showed that blind graduates were higher unemployment rate and having positive community adjustment.

Weiner (1991) described the Social Support Net work of 55 blind young adults. Arizona Social Support Inventory Scale and Net work Analysis Profile were used to examine the key aspects of net work structure and to evaluate the attributes of net work links. The result of this study indicated that with the exception of net work size, the level of visual impairment may have less impact on net work structure than such factors as age of onset of blindness, type of school attended, acceptance of blindness, marital status, gender and mastery.

(iii) Concept Formation

Carnoldi (1992) studied the visuo- spatial imagery capacity of blind and sighted to follow an imaginary pathway through three dimension matrices of different complexity. The blind subjects appeared to use specific visuo-spatial process in the task, but they had difficulty with dimensional matrix on the other hand, when a three dimensional pattern exceeded sighted capacity, the blind and sighted children showed similar pattern of errors. Further analysis suggested that both visuo-spatial processes and verbal modification were used for both group's subjects.

Coleman (1991) studied the concept of length in blind children. The concept of length was investigated by use of Fair Assessment Devices (FAD). The FAD included the fair assessment in relation to concept of length i.e. conservation of length, transitivity of length, written length assessment and functional length assessment. Both qualitative and quantitative data were obtained on all the assessment. The samples were comprised 7 braille readers, 7 large print readers and 10 regular print readers. The results revealed that the regular print readers had the least difficulty with the task, large print reader and braille print reader have more difficulty to attain the concept of length.

Rosan (1981) studied Spatial Gait Pattern of congenitally blind and normally sighted children. The sample consisted of 20 congenitally blind and 29 sighted children. Selected components of Spatial Gait Patterns (Speed, Strides length, Step length, Stride width, Foot-angle and Arm swing) were assessed using a combination of observation and Footprint Recording Methodologies. Result showed that sighted children demonstrated specific characteristics of spatial gait pattern with greater consistency.

Kuzntsova (1993) studied the tactile thresholds on the palm surface of finger pads, using stimulation with ultrasound focused. The samples consisted 20 normal and 43 blind children. Result finds that the normal children are higher on tactile sensitivity in comparison to blind children. Tactile sensitivity decreases with age in normal children as well as in blind ones, if they lost their vision less than two years ago. Tactile sensitivity of blind children since childhood remains constant after the age of thirty years.

Woo (1990) studied the perception with moving objects of blind children and normal children. Twenty five blind children with no other additional handicap and twenty five normal children were included in the sample. Results indicate that blind children have no main effect for accommodation grouping but a main effect was revealed for object direction in blind children.

(iv) Emotional Development

Minter and Pring (1992) designed a study to recognizing vocal expression of emotion and recognizing the sound of non emotional objects. The study was conducted on a sample of eight congenitally blind children and eight sighted children. A audio tape which containing verbal and nonverbal emotional sounds, was used. The results concluded that sighted children did not differ in ability to recognize non emotional sounds, but blind children were less able to identify the emotions sounds.

Date-Kwan-Jamie and Hughes (1991) identified specific aspects of Home environment related to development of visually impaired children. The findings revealed that over all Home environment were found to be consistently favourable despite the differences in the parent's Socio-economic Status Emotional and verbal responsiveness of visually impaired children were significantly related with Home environment.

(v) Language Development

Erin (1986) examined question frequency and type in language sample from 36 sighted and blind children (Blind, low vision, and sighted group). ANOVA results demonstrated no significant difference among the blind and sighted; and groups of low vision and sighted in the ratio of questions asked for each 100 alternate. These differences are occurred with some minor distinction type usage by age and visual function.

McCounchil, and Morre (1994) compared the early language of blind and additional handicapped blind children using the Reynell Zinken Development Scale. The assessment was repeated at the 6-8 months interval. Further information on milestones and content of early expressive language was obtained from parents during recording of their children's expressive language development occurred later that of sighted children. The effects of children having even a small amount of vision could discern in their early words. No correlation was found between expressive language level and sensorimotor understanding.

2. INDIAN STUDIES

(i) Academic Achievements and Intelligence

Singh (1985) compared the intelligence of visually handicapped adult trainees, students and staff members of National Institute of Visually Handicapped, Dehradun (NIVH). Weschler's Verbal Adults Intelligence Scale was used for data collection. The findings revealed that Blind did not differ significantly from the sighted on Intelligence. Results demonstrated that congenitally blind and adventitiously blind differed significantly on intelligence sub-test scores.

Nisar (1990) conducted a study to find out the psychological problems of congenital and adventitious visually impaired in relation to their academic attainment. The Edward Personality Questionnaire has been used to measure the psychological problems of the visually impaired children studying in Ahmadi Blind School, Aligarh. The main findings of the study are: (i) Congenitally blinds are more extrovert than their counterparts; (ii) The congenitally blind children have been found superior in academic performance than the adventitiously blind children; (iii) Academic achievement of both groups are not affected by psychological problems as well as extroversion.

Bhardwaj, R. (1997) conducted a comparative study on Adequate depth of feeling and sex as correlates of the need for achievement among handicapped and non-handicapped children. The sample comprised 600 children of both sex (boys and girls). Out of these, 200 children were cerebral palsied, 200 children were congenitally blind and 200 children were normal, but the final sample of 240 children were selected through multi staged sampling technique. The tools used to collect the data were Emotional Competencies Scale by Sharma and Bharadwaj, and Personal Preference Schedule by Tripathi. The results of this indicate that the cerebral palsied children had greater need for achievement in those boys who were imbuild with high level of adequate depth of feeling in comparison to congenitally visually impaired children.

Reddy, G.L. and Rajaguru, S. (1998) conducted a study on Divergent thinking, Convergent thinking and Mental ability of Congenital Blind children. The study was conducted on a sample of 64 congenital visually impaired children from 19 integrated schools and 2 special schools of Tamilnadu. The Divergent Thinking Test and Convergent Thinking Test in Braille form and Mental Ability Test were used. The result revealed that the variables such as sex, residence, type of school, parent's education, parents' occupation and family size were least shown impact on divergent thinking of congenital visually impaired children. Congenital blind children with illiterate parents have better convergent thinking. Positive correlation between divergent thinking and mental ability and convergent thinking and mental ability were found.

(ii) Adjustment

Kaur, Singh and Jain (1984) made an attempt to study the social adjustment of normal and blind adolescents. The sample consisted of 80 normal adolescents compared with 40 blind adolescents in the age-group of 11-16 years. The tools used were:

Junior Personality Inventory and Personal Information Sheet. The results showed no significant difference among the sighted and blind adolescents in relation to social adjustment.

William (1988) compared the extent of adjustment of blind and deaf children. The sample comprised all the special school of Mysore, Hubli, Gulbarga and Banglore. 51 blind and 65 deaf children of class V-VIII formed the sample. The researcher has used Pre- Adolescents Adjustment Scale (PAAS) by Udai Pareek. The major findings were (i) Both the blind and deaf children had a good level of home adjustment; (ii) in the case of adjustment with peers, both the blind and deaf were well adjusted with their peers; (iii) Blind children had a low level of adjustment with their teachers; (iv) In the area of general adjustment, the blind showed better adjustment than the deaf.

Sarita (1985) conducted a comparative study on adjustment pattern of blind and sighted children. The sample comprised of 40 visually handicapped and 40 sighted children. The finding of the study showed that over-all emotional, social and educational adjustment of visually handicapped was poor than the sighted students. Pal, Nigam (2000) conducted a comparative study of adjustment of blind children of general , SC and ST caste category. The sample comprised of 100 blind children of various caste. The Adjustment Inventory by Sinha & Singh were used. The results showed that general caste students was better adjustment than the SC and ST students.

(iii) Anxiety

Sharma (1990) conducted a study to find out the anxiety level of visually handicapped and normal children. The study was conducted on a sample of 50 visually handicapped and 40 sighted students of class IV-IX standards of Aligarh district in U.P. The General Anxiety Scale for Children (GASC) and Test Anxiety Scale for Children (TASC) by Kumar were used earlier. The results revealed that visually handicapped children were significantly more anxious than the sighted children. They were found more anxious for their examination than their seeing counterparts.

Zaidi (1985) conducted a study on General Anxiety and Test Anxiety of blind and normal children belonging to 6th and 7th grades. The finding showed that Blind children did not differ significantly on test anxiety.

Ghai and Sen (1985) studied work adjustment and job anxiety of different categories of the handicapped in open employment. The sample consisted of 30 blinds, 35 deaf, 30 orthopaedically handicapped and 30 normal adults. The work adjustment was assessed by Rikard Palmer's Work Adjustment Schedule and Job Anxiety was assessed by Sinha's Job Anxiety Questionnaire. The results showed that the deaf had the best work adjustment than the blinds. In respect to job anxiety the study has revealed a higher job anxiety level for the disabled, the blinds having the highest mean anxiety score followed by the deaf and orthopaedically handicapped.

(iv) Creativity

Kamila (1986) compared the Creative thinking of blind and normal children in Bhubneshwar (Orissa). Acharulu's Thinking Creativity Test Battery was used for data collection. The finding of study revealed that the normal children tend to score significantly higher than the blind children on all the three creative abilities viz. fluency, flexibility and originality and the creativity has positive correlation with scholastic achievement.

Sidique (1989) conducted a study on creative potential of Blind children in relation to their socio-economic status. The tools used were: Verbal Test of Creative Thinking (Baqer Mehdi) and Socio-Economic Status Scale (Kuppuswamy), the results of the study revealed that: (i) High Socio-economic group was higher in creative potential; (ii) Children coming from the urban area have more creative potential in comparison to children coming from rural area; (iii) Blind boys were found much more creative than the blind girls; (iv) Highly creative Blind children belong to educated families while low creative children come from uneducated families.

Arora, S.(2000) conducted a comparative study of creative

Potential of congenitally and adventitiously blind children. The sample consisted of 50 congenitally blind and 50 adventitiously blind children. Questionnaire on Socio-economic Status Scale and Verbal Test of Creativity were administered. Result show that adventitiously visually- impaired group shows better development of flexibility and originality in comparison to congenitally blind children.

Arora, S. (2000) made a study of creative of congenitally impaired children. For this purpose a sample of 50 congenitally blind children (25 boys and 25 girls) were selected. General Information Questionnaire and Verbal Test of Creative thinking by Baquer Mehndi were used for data collection. Finding of the study revealed that congenitally blind children were poor creative potential. Boys of CB group are more superior and creative potential and its component like fluency, flexibility and originality.

(v) Education

Shukla (1983) conducted the research on the attitude of blind towards integrated education and reported that the most of the blind experts do not possess the positive attitude towards integrated education programme. They are of the opinion that separate and need based education should be planned for visually handicapped children.

Dixit (1985) investigated the blind education for a period of one decade with respect to organisational structure, percentage of beneficiaries, sex-wise average number of pupil per school, pupil-teacher ratio percentage of trained and various services provided in blind schools. The analysis showed an over all percentage increased with respect to their characteristics except for the percentage of school employing Integrated System of Education to a remarkable point and providing training in various vocational trades along with regular teaching. It was observed that while schools for the sighted have been doubled during the last three years, the schools for the blinds have increased by about 3-1/2 times during the same period. Similarly for school enrollment 40 percent increase was found for sighted and an increase of 200 percent for the blind. drop out percentage was found less in blind than in normal schools, class-wise enrollment was also slightly better at initial stages. The problem of 'Geographic accessibility' was also highlighted in this study.

Sangeeta, (1996), made a comparative study of the learning aptitudes of the congenitally and adventitiously blind pupils. The sample of the study comprised 50 blind subjects, which consisted of 25 children each from congenitally and adventitiously blind groups. They belonged to the residential school for blind in Haryana and Chandigarh. The subjects were selected randomly. Tools used to collect the data were Indian adaptation of Newland's Blind Learning Aptitude Test (BLAT) by Singh and Sati. The result of the study reflect that: (i) Learning aptitude of the adventitiously and congenitally blind students differed significantly. (ii) The congenitally and adventitiously blind students also did not differ significantly in the time taken for test completion on BLAT.

Punani, B. (1997) compared the evaluation of the effectiveness of various modes of education of blind children. The sample comprised 130 blind children, of these 50 children were from integrated education, 26 were from semi integrated education and 54 from residential schools. Their age ranged between 10 to 15 years, who were studying in class IV, V and VI. The table used to collect the data included Tooze Braille Speed Test, Vineland Social Maturity Scale, and Mani's Test of Concept Development. The results indicated that

(i) Integrated education was found much more effective than residential education.

(ii) Integrated education emerged the most effective in attracting children from farming community, farm labourers and families engaged in craft.

(iii) Integrated education failed to enhance social integration of the blind children. Even in respect of social maturity, it has no inbuilt advantage over other modes of education.

(iv) Its quality on education in terms of speed and accuracy of braille is comparatively inferior.

(vi) Personality

Bhargava and Lavania (1981) worked on comparative study of personality factors of sensory disabled and normal children having same age and sex. Both the groups were matched in respect of Socio-economic status. Kapoor's Socio-Economic Status Scale and Rao's Children Personality Questionnaire were used. The result showed that the sensory disabled were more reserved, emotionally unstable, shy, dependent, sentimental, secure and relaxed than their counterparts i.e. the normal children.

Singh and Pathak (1984) compared the blind with the sighted on four personality dimensions : Psychoticism (P), Extroversion (E), Neuroticism (N) and the Lie Score (L) as postulated by Eysenck and Eysenck. Results indicated that the groups did not differ significantly in any of the four scales, though there was some marginal difference in the lie scores between the groups; the blinds having the higher scores. This suggested that the comparatively blinds responded to the lie items in a more socially desirable manner.

Kapoor and Sen (1984) made a comparative study of the congenitally and the adventitiously blind and their sighted peers on some personality variables. The study was confined to 27 congenitally blind, 11 adventitiously blind and 27 sighted children. The tools used were Maundsley Personality Inventory by Jalota and Kapoor and Schaie's Personality Perceptual Rigidity Questionnaire. The results indicated that the congenitally and adventitiously blind groups do not differ significantly from each other or from their sighted peers on the personality variables, emotional stability perceptual rigidity and social responsibility.

Goel and Sen (1985) have reported a few studies which were carried out recently in the context of personality dimension of the visually handicapped by several students of psychology.

The result showed a large number of the subjects have poor self-concept and emotional stability; below average intelligence; and physical dependence. They were found to be not fully congnisant of reality and possessed a sense of insecurity. They were rated by their teachers as aggressive, uninhibited, generally group-dependent, sociable, predictable and emotionally maladjusted, the blinds also showed less inter individual variance in terms of skills.

Bhatnagar (1985) studied 50 blind and 50 sighted students studying in middle and high special schools. Meenakshi's Personality Inventory, Sinha's Anxiety Scale, Attitude Scale and Security-Insecurity Test were used for data collection. The main findings of the study were: (i) The sighted children were higher than the blind children on achievement, exhibitionism, autonomy, dominance, endurance and aggression. Similarly the blind children were higher on affiliation, abasement and nurturance; (ii) The blinds were significantly more anxious and dependent and the sighted were significantly more relaxed and independent in comparison to each other.

Rath (1988) has analyzed and compared the personality dynamics of blind and sighted students. The sample consisted of 125 blind and 125 sighted students of class IX to XII. The tools used were Hindi version of the Minnesota Counselling Inventory (MCI) and SES Scale (Kuppuswamy). The result showed that the blind subjects were less adjusted on the dimensions of family relationship, emotional stability, adjustment to reality, mood and conformity in comparison to sighted students.

Reddy, N.Y. (1997) made of a comparative study of the orthopaedically handicapped, visually handicapped and hearing impaired children on some personality correlates. The study was confined to 838 boys and 122 girls. The sample were selected through incidental sampling technique. The tools and techniques used to collect the data included Open Ended Interview Schedule, Disabled Adjustment Inventory, and Dutt's Personality Inventory. The main findings of the study were: (i) The visually handicapped confront maximum number of problems of adjustment in areas like school, home, social issues, self-confidence and feeling of inferiority . (ii) Orthopaedically handicapped were found to be much better than the visually handicapped but worse than the speech and hearing impaired in adjustment. (iii) There were no sex differences among the groups as far as problems of adjustment were concerned.

Arora, S. (2000) conducted a study on Personality configuration on congenitally blind children. For this purpose a sample of 50 congenitally blind children (25 boys and 25 girls) from VIII-X class were selected from various special children. 16 Personality factor Questionnaire, Socio Economic Status Scale and General Information Questionnaire were used. Result shows that congenitally blind children were characterized by the quality of easy going, imaginative shrewd with superior ego strength.

(vii) Value and Mannerism

Jayasree (1982) conducted a comparative study of the manneristic behaviour of the blind and the sighted children. Manneristic behaviour is often required as a mechanism for coping with anxiety and also regarded as a tension-release mechanism. Four kinds of mechanism (head movement, eye-poking and rubbing, clapping and jumping) were found to exist only in the blind children. The sighted children showed 13 other types of mannerisms in higher percentage than that of the blind children. But blind girls showed more mannerism in comparison to blind boys.

Sinha (1985) studied value pattern of blind and sighted adults. Sample consisted of 50 blind and 50 sighted children. The finding of this study reveal that blind adults were superior on religious, economic and moral values than the sighted. Blind children are more religious and affixed trust on religious practices. The most significant differences were existing the scores of blind and sighted in relation to aesthetic value, sighted were more aesthetic than the blind children.

OVERVIEW OF THE CHAPTER

Research in special education as a subject of independent existence in the literature on educational research is a recent development. In India, this area has received attention only in 1990 (Buch, 1990). An overview of related literature reveals low yield of researches in the field. Only 15 Ph.D's are available in Indian context alongwith six other comparative studies on blind and normal children. Table 2.1 gives an exhaustive dimensional analysis of the researches on visual impairment conducted in India and abroad.

Table 2.1 : Dimensional Analysis of Studies on Blind in India and Abroad (Upto Dec. 1994)

S.No.	*Dimensions of visual impairment*	*Ph.D's*		*Research Papers*		*Unpublished Indian Dissertations*
		Indian	*Foreign*	*Indian*	*Foreign*	
1.	Achievement	1	1	3	-	1
2.	Adjustment	1	3	3	1	1
3.	Anxiety	-	-	11	3	1
4.	Concept Formation	4	1	8	2	-
5.	Creativity	1	-	1	2	1
6.	Education	2	1	13	2	-
7.	Intelligence	1	1	3	1	-
8.	Kinesthetic Movement	-	-	3	-	-
9.	Memory	1	2	1	1	1
10.	Personality	4	4	3	3	1
11.	Rehabilitation	2	4	12	4	-
12.	*Miscellaneous*	*3*	*3*	*21*	*2*	*1*
	Total	16	20	82	21	7

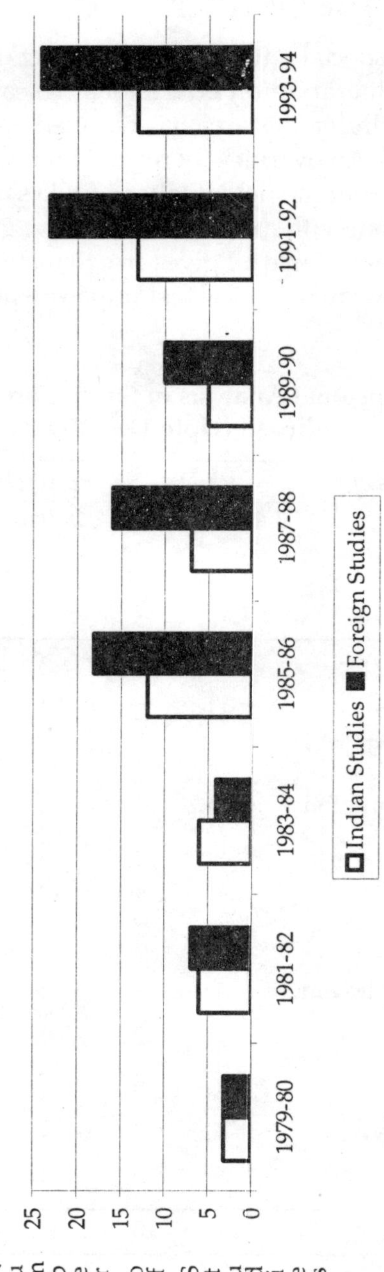

Fig. 2: A Comparative Graph in the Field of Visual Impairment

The year-wise trend of growth and development of researches in the field show spurt in foreign perspective since (1985-86). This year has also witnessed a sharp rise in India, the year of formation of National Policy on Education, 1986. Indian scenario since then marked by the plateau in research efforts. This apathetic attitude of researchers may be due to the reason that subject has remained in the backyard, as special education, especially activities in the field of visual impairment have been conducted outside the mainstream of education for a long time. The institutional infrastructure available for research in this area has also remained inadequate. Thus, research in the field of visual impairment is only in an embryonic stage with negligible amount of research done at the doctoral level or in projects. Due to the lack of efforts in organizational planning researches on visually impairment exhibit an imbalance and scattered nature.

The establishment of National Institute of Visually Handicapped (NIVH) and research organizations like NCERT, ICSSR, UGC, RCI and NIEPA has improved the range and quality of research activities in the field of education of the disabled. Activities in this direction by NCERT, NIEPA, NPE, IEP, POA, RIC, NIVH are rapidly gaining momentum in this direction, thus fulfilling the provisions of equal opportunity in education; vocation and social status in the country's constitution.

3

DESIGN OF THE STUDY

The research problem has been formulated in the preceding pages. In this chapter, the design of the study is set under the following heads:

Sample

Tools and Techniques

Transcription of the tools

Administration of the tools

Collection of data

Statistical procedures

SAMPLE

The present study deals with the two types of samples i.e. blind and normal children respectively. The researcher has conveniently classified the sampling process into the following phases:

i. First Phase of Sampling

It is basically concerned with the selection of blind children. The researcher has selected 100 blind children (50 congenitally and 50 adventitiously blind children). The systematic randomization technique has been adopted in order to get the appropriate sample from these institutions. The sample comprises of the VIII, IX and X grades and in the age group of

13-18+ years respectively. The table 3.1 shows the distribution of cases according to type of visual impairment and institution.

Table 3.1: The Distribution of the Cases of Blind Children in Special School

S.No.	*Institution/Types of visual impairment*	*Congenital*		*Adventitious*		*Total*
		Boys	*Girls*	*Boys*	*Girls*	
1.	Ahmadi Blind School A.M.U. Aligarh	4	3	3	2	12
2.	Model School for Blind NIVH Dehradun	7	7	12	10	36
3.	Govt. Boys Blind School, Delhi.	14	-	10	-	24
4.	Rashtriya Virjan Andh Kanya Vidhyalaya New Delhi.	-	15	-	13	28
	Total	25	25	25	25	100

ii. Second Phase of Sampling

This phase of sampling deals with the selection of normal children from the similar geographical locale as of blind children. The sample consists of 100 children (50 boys and 50 girls) from different schools through Systematic randomization technique. This sample includes the students of VIII, IX and X grades in the age group of 13-18+ years.

Table 3.2: The Distribution of the Cases of Normal Children

S.No.	*Institution*	*Boys*	*Girls*	*Total*
1.	Abdullah Girls College A.M.U. Aligarh	-	20	20
2.	DAV College, Dehradun	15	-	25
3.	Central School, Delhi	25	15	35
4.	Agra Public School, Agra	10	15	15
	Total	50	50	100

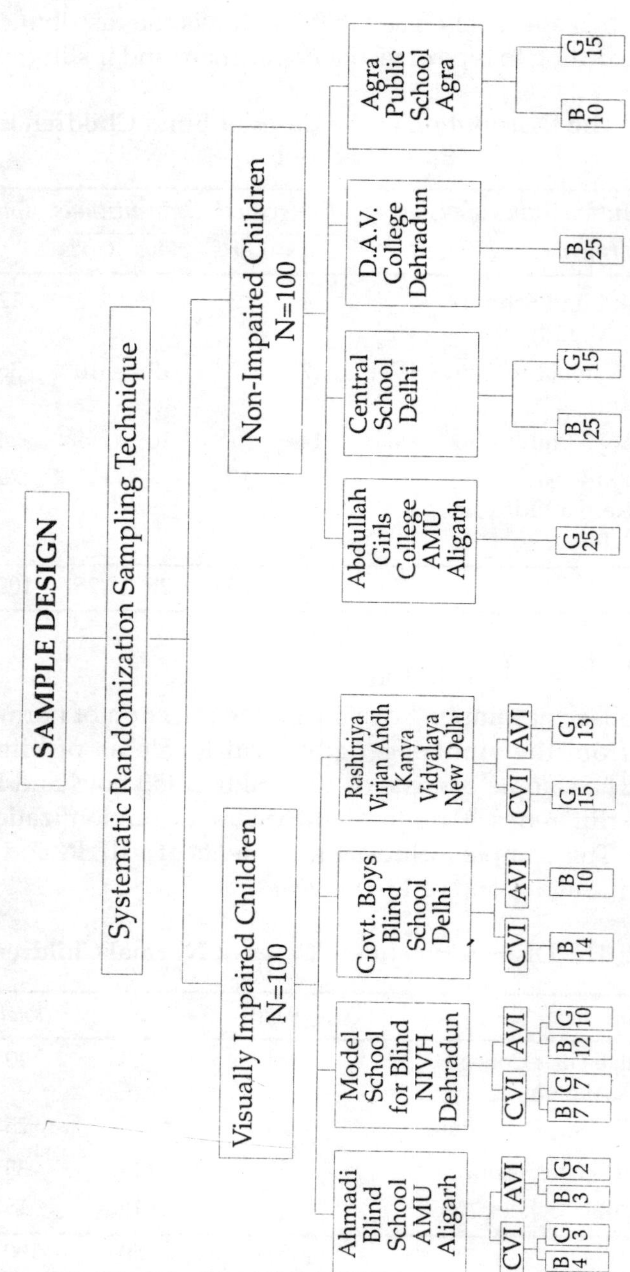

Fig. 3: Flow Chart Showing the Sampling Procedure of the Present Study

MATCHING TECHNIQUES EMPLOYED

With a view to evaluate experimental findings and to emphasize the psychological differences between the two groups, it was decided to equate the two groups on some variables. Considering the diversity of the groups the equating was done only as far as possible, for a perfect equating is an impossibility. Ackoff (1953) rightly remarked that, "*the variables used should be such as will be useful in the specific situations manipulations of all the variables is not possible. Hence research must be determined in situations which differ from the idealized one*". For these reasons only those variables which could be manipulated and were found to be useful were controlled. These variables are: (1) Age (2) Grade and (3) Socio-economic status.

(1) Age

Many studies have indicated the influence of age upon the personality as well as on creativity of both blind and normal children. Many personality factors like emotions, interest, adjustment, aggression, I.Q., anxiety and creativity are directly related to the age of the individual. This point has been emphasized by Kaur (1984), Kopperman (1985), Parsons (1989), Blanksky (1992). For the purpose of matching the two groups, the researcher has computed the chi-square.

Table 3.3: Distribution of Cases According to Age

S.NO.	*AGE/GROUP*	*13-15*	*15-17*	*17-18+*	*TOTAL*
1.	Blind Children	30	34	36	100
2.	Normal Children	40	35	25	100
	Total	70	69	61	200

$X^2 = 1.99$; df = 02; P= Not significant

The calculated chi-square value in the three different age-groups are found non-significant between blind and normal children. It confirms that the groups under consideration are homogeneous in relation to age groups. Hence, it can be confirmed that the groups are almost equal and matched to each other.

(2) Grade

The two groups have also been equated as far as possible in respect of grades. The following table shows the distribution of cases according to grades:-

Table 3.4: Distribution of Cases According to Grade

S.No.	*GRADE/GROUP*	*VIII*	*IX*	*X*	*TOTAL*
1.	Blind Children	50	31	19	100
2.	Normal Children	47	27	26	100
	Total	97	58	45	200

$X^2 = 1.42$ df= 2; P = Not significant

The chi-square value given in the above table is found non-significant at the 0.05 level, indicating that there is no significant difference between the two groups under consideration in relation to their grades. This confirms that the matching of the groups on various grades is satisfactory and adequate.

(3) Socio-Economic Status

Socio economic status appears to be resultant of the position of an individual in a society by virtue of a complex fusion of both the social and economic positions which often do not run parallel. This intermingling takes place in an undefined and curious manner eventually presenting a complex indicator to socio-economic status. Socio-economic status has been retained as an effective measure in terms of the occupation of father as confirmed by Tyler (1965), Kuppuswami (1962), Getal (1989), in addition to education, income caste, culture etc. Behavioural differences in blind children may also be due to differences in socio-economic status.

Socio-economic status influences values differences in home management, husband-wife relationship and child-rearing habits (Sharma, 1979). It may also favour the development of intelligence as favoured by Fryer (1922), Richards (1963), Shanthamani (1990). Thus the socio-economic status is an important sociological variable affecting the personality and creativity of an individual. To Match the sample with regard to socio-economic status researcher computed the chi-square value as given in the Table 3.5.

Table 3.5: Distribution of Cases According to Socio-Economic Status

S.No.	*SES/GROUP*	*H*	*M*	*L*	*TOTAL*
1.	Blind	09	71	20	100
2.	NI	15	67	18	100
	Total	24	138	38	200

$X^2 = 1.72$ df= 2; P = Not significant

The application of chi-square test on the distribution of cases on three SES-groups i.e. H, M and L revealed that there exists no significant difference between blind and normal children. The value of chi-square for this table has been found to be non-significant at 0.05 level. This confirms that the blind and NI groups are equated in respect to socio-economic status.

TOOLS AND TECHNIQUES

Having selected the sample, the next task was to choose suitable tool for the collection of data. The selection of tool for a particular study depends upon various considerations such as the objectives of the study, the amount of time at the disposal of the researcher, availability of suitable tests, personal competence of the researcher to administer, score and interpret the test results and the like. Taking into consideration these factors a carefully selected tests were used to find out and compare the personality factors and creative potential of two groups viz. blind and normal children. The following tools were included in the test battery.

a) Preliminary Tool

The researcher has developed a preliminary tool which put the research in action. Thus to make the conducive environment to work with blind and normal population and for probing into their private world, the researcher has given it the name as General Information Questionnaire. Its transcribed script i.e. Braille has been employed with blind children and Devanagari script with normal children.

b) Matching Tool

The researcher has equalized the blind and normal children on Socio-economic status. The Socio-economic Status Scale by Dr. S.P. Kulshreshtha has been employed for this purpose.

c) Main Tools of the Study

The tools and techniques employed for final collection of data in order to achieve the objectives are categorized under this category. These tool are as following:

Sixteen Personality Factor Questionnaire (1973)

It is originally developed by Dr. R.B. Cattell and adopted by Dr. S.D. Kapoor in Hindi version to measure the 16 Personality Factors.

Verbal Test of Creativity, (1985)

This tool was prepared by Prof. Baquer Mehdi to measure the creative potential of the blind and normal children.

The use of the above tools is elaborated below in order to justify their selection and application particularly with the special population of the blind children.

General Information Questionnaire (GIQ)

To understand the complex nature of personality of an

individual, which is the product of a number of psycho-social forces, it is necessary to know the background of the individual. This information is also very helpful in scoring and interpreting the responses of main tools. For collecting relevant information on various background factors, the researcher has employed self-constructed questionnaire, which provides information regarding subject's name, age, caste, class, sex, section, father's occupation, family (Urban/Rural) etc.

The information gathered so far gave an exposure and insight to the researcher in interpretation of the responses of the 16 Personality factors and Creative potential of the blind and normal children.

Socio-economic Status Scale (SESS)

Socio-economic status scale is the ranking of an individual by the society in which he lives in terms of his material belongings and cultural possessions along with the degree of respect, power and influence, he wields. In the present study the researcher used the Socio-economic Status Scale (SESS) developed by Dr. S.P. Kulshreshtha (1980). This is a quite reliable and valid tool having workability with both type of sample under consideration.

Sixteen Personality Factor Questionnaire (16PF)

The sixteen Personality Factor Questionnaire is most popular questionnaire for personality assessment. The Sixteen PF Questionnaire is an objectively scorable test devised to give the most complete coverage of personality, possible in a brief time. The test was designed in Form A, B, C and D respectively. In this study Form-D is used because it has lesser items of each factor and less time-consuming (25-35 minutes). The questions are arranged in cyclic order to determine by the plan to give interest for the examinee. The scores can be used for educational and industrial prediction and clinical diagnosis.

This test was originally developed by Dr. R.B. Cattell (1973) and adopted by Dr. S.D. Kapoor in Hindi version. This tool is comprehensive and attempts to probe the personality through 16 Personality Factors. Each factor is listed with its Alphabetic designation and description of low and high scores. The 16 PF's are mentioned in the table as given.

Table 3.6: High and Low Sten Score Description of the 16 Personality Factors

Sl. No.	*Low Sten Score Description*	*High Sten Score Description*
1. A	Reserved, detached, critical, aloof Stiff	Outgoing, warmhearted, easygoing participating
	Sizothymia	Affectothymia
2. B	Dull	Bright
	Low intelligence	High intelligence
3. C	Affected by feeling, emotionally less stable, easily upset, changeable	Emotionally stable, mature, faces reality, calm
	Lower ego strength	Higher ego strength
4. E	Humble, mild, easily led, docile, accommodating	Assertive, aggressive, competitive, stubborn
	Submissiveness	Dominance
5. F	Sober, tacitum, serious	Happy-go-lucky, enthusiastic
	Desurgency	Surgency
6. G	Expedient, disregards rules	Conscientious, persistent, moralistic staid
	Weaker super-ego strength	stronger superego strength
7. H	Shy, timid, threat-sensitive	Venturesome, uninhibited, socially bold
	Threctia	Parima

Sl. No.	*Low Sten Score Description*	*High Sten Score Description*
8. I	Tough-minded, self-reliant realistic	Tender-minded, sensitive, clinging overprotected
	Harnia	Premsia
9. L	Trusting, accepting conditions	Suspicious, hard to fool
	Alaxia	Protension
10. M	Practical, "Down-to-earth" concerns	Imaginative, bohemian, absent-minded
	Praxemia	Autia
11. N	Forthright, unpretentious, genius but socially clumsy	Astute, polished, socially aware
	Artlessness	Shrewdness
12. O	Self-assured, placid, secure, complacent, serene	Apprehensive, self-reproaching, insecure worrying, troubled
	Untroubled adequacy	Guilt proneness
13. Q1	Conservative, respecting traditional ideas	Experimenting, liberal, free-thinking
	Conservatism of temperament	Radicalism
14. Q2	Group dependent, a "joiner" and sound follower	Self-sufficiency, resourceful, prefers own decisions
	Group adherence	Self-sufficiency
15. Q3	Undisciplined, self-conflict lax, follows own urges, careless of social rules	Controlled, exacting will power Socially precise, compulsive, following self-image
	Low self-sentiment integration	High strength of self-sentiment
16. Q4	Relaxed, tranquil, torpid, untrusted, composed	Tense, frustrated, drive, overqrought
	Low ergic tension	High ergic tension

VERBAL TEST OF CREATIVITY

The verbal test of creative thinking is part of the total battery which consists of both verbal and non-verbal tests. This test is prepared particularly for the Northern Indian populations and moreover, this test employed as culture-free test. Verbal test of creativity is reliable and valid tool in the research studies conducted in the area of creativity. It can be safely used for identifying creative talent from middle school and going upto the graduate level in blind and normal population. This test comprises of the following sub-tests:

(a) Consequence Test

The consequences test consists of three hypothetical situations:

(a) What would happen if man could fly like birds?

(b) What would happen if our school had wheels? and

(c) What would happen if man does not have any need for food?

The subject is required to think as many consequences of these situations as one can, and write them under each situation in the space provided. The situations being hypothetical, minimize the effect of experience and also provide the subjects with an unlimited opportunity to make responses. The test encourages free play of imagination and originality. An example is given on the test booklet to acquaint the subjects with the nature of the test. The time allowed for the three problems is 4 minutes each.

(b) Unusual Test

This test presents the subjects with the names of three common objects- a piece of stone, a wooden stick and water and requires him to write as many novel, interesting and unusual uses of these objects as he may think of. The example given on the test booklet properly acquaints the subjects with the nature of the task. This test measures the subject's ability to retrieve items of information from his personal information in storage. Evidently, it also measures the subject's ability to shift frames of reference to use the environment in an original manner. The time allowed for the three task is 5 minutes each.

(c) New Relationships Test

This test presents the subjects with three pairs of words apparently different, tree and houses, chair and ladder, air and water and requires him to think and write as many novel relationships as possible between the two objects of each pair in the space provided, the test provides an opportunity for the free play of an imagination and originality. The time allowed for each pair of words is 5 minutes.

(4) Product Improvement Test

In this test the subject is asked to think of a simple wooden toy of a horse and suggest addition of new things to it, to make it more interesting for the children to play. The time allowed is 6 minutes.

TRANSCRIPTION OF THE TOOLS IN BRAILLE

In order to create conducive and least resistance environment to the blind sample, the researcher has get transcribed all the tools viz. GIQ; SESS; and 16 PF and Verbal Test of Creativity into Braille formats. The researcher got wholehearted support of the Manager, Central Braille Press, NIVH, Dehradun and some other voluntary charitable agencies working for blinds at Vrindavan, Mathura. Moreover the blind children were allowed to give their answers in Braille. It gave them more confidence and conformity in probing of their deeper personality as it adhere to the rules of privacy of responses.

ADMINISTRATION OF THE TOOLS

Administration of tools is divided into two phases i.e. matching phase and final phase.

Phase I: Administration of Tools for Matching Purposes on Primary Sample

In order to establish rapport and develop a conducive environment General Information Questionnaire was administered. The questionnaire proves a clue to assessing the future personality of the subjects. It creates a friendly atmosphere among the tester and the testee and inspires the isolated groups of blind children to express themselves freely. This test helps in assessing the background of sample as well as their interests, ambitions, behaviour and opinions etc. For matching on socio-economic status, the Socio-Economic Status Scale (SESS) prepared by Dr. S.P. Kulshreshtha was administered for equalizing the status of blind and normal children. Due care was taken to administer the test in a friendly atmosphere and the students were assured that the information provided by them would be kept confidential. The SES assigns an approximate weightage to the responses given by the students.

Phase II: Administration of Main Tools on the Final Sample

In this phase actual tests are administered for personality assessment and measurement of creative potential of blind and normal children.

The researcher made all favourable attempts to establish a rapport and create an encouraging atmosphere with the blind children by greeting them warmly and talking to them in a friendly manner. The test administration involves physical preparations such as seating arrangement, watching the subject's expressions etc.

Secondly, the test of creative potential prepared by Prof. Baquer Mehdi was administered for measuring creativity. The researcher read out all the necessary instructions to the students before they started writing their responses. The blind children were allowed to write through Braille language. A sufficient time is given to each group for completing the test.

COLLECTION OF DATA

The collection of data from the selected institutions is the major portion of the research work. It may be very difficult to obtain data from the blind subjects because of communication problems and because they do not readily mix with other normal or new individuals out of isolated feelings and inferiority complexes. Principals of all these institutions were approached and the objectives and utility of the research project were explained to them. The principals and the staff of all these institutions took a keen interest and they provided all the necessary facilities and time which made the test administration and data collection an expedient process and a wonderful experience. The class-teachers' assistance was sought whenever needed. Before collecting the data the researcher has visited the special schools a couple of times and had friendly discussions with the students to overcome communication problems and win their acceptance.

The researcher gave a short introduction to the students about the research, it was designed to study their personality and creative potential, and that the result would be beneficial in improving their learning and academic conditions. After decoding the responses of various tests with the help of braille experts and braille workers researcher entered into the phase of scoring and statistical computation.

STATISTICAL PROCEDURES

The following statistical procedures were adopted for the analysis of data:

(1) The raw scores of the blind and normal children on the 16 Personality Factor Questionnaire and Verbal Test of Creativity were tabulated separately in to frequency distributions and means and standard deviations were calculated according to the usual formula.

(2) Comparison between blind and normal groups on the personality factors and creative potential were made on the basis of CR test. The CR test was used to find

out differences between uncorrelated means in two samples of equal size.

(3) Comparison between the adventitious and congenital blind boys and girls on the study of personality factors and creative potential were made on the basis of 't' test. The 't' test was used to find out the differences between uncorrelated means in to small samples of equal size.

(4) Chi-square as a test of significance was applied to find out differences in background factors, namely Age, Grade and Socio-economic status respectively. The confidence level establish in this test were the same as the in the case of the 't' test i.e. 0.05 and 0.01.

OVERVIEW OF THE CHAPTER

In this chapter, the design of the study has been laid down. A sequential schedule of the steps involved are given and the systematic randomization method of sampling is found suitable for the Non-impaired and Visually- impaired population. An equitable distribution of sexwise and on set of impairment are chosen (Table 3.1 & 3.2).

The different tests used for matching purpose are described. The justified the 16 PF Questionnaire and Verbal Test of Creativity as the most suitable for measuring the personality and creative potential of blind and NI children. All these tools are most sophisticated and highly reliable and valid hence these are compatible and feasible with the samples in hand. To avoid the burden some bulk of manual content, the researcher has not discussed the physical and technical qualities of these tools in detail.

The next chapter present the analysis and interpretation of the personality factors and results have been derived.

4

PERSONALITY DEVELOPMENT OF BLIND AND NORMAL CHILDREN

The present chapter deals with the analysis and interpretation of the data collected through 16 PF in order to achieve the basic objectives of the study, the detailed statistical results in the form of 'CR' and 't' values have been given in tabular form along with their subsistence interpretation. The major objectives of the present study is to study the personality factors of blind and normal children and to compare the personality factor of congenitally blind and Adventitiously blind children. To achieve these objectives along with the subsidiary objective to gender discrimination, the author has exhibited the statistical operation in the following tables. It leads to another extraction of the personality factors and make it crystal clear through vivid interpretations.

The table 4.1 reveals that the computed CR values among the various groups under study are found 4.65; 2.46; and 2.30 respectively. While the boys and girls separately as well as combinedly show the significant differences between blind and normal group in relation to personality factor - 'A'. The mean of sten scores in case of BB and BG (7.10-6.04) are showing expoversive trends in their personality and found distinctly superior in relation to outgoing factor. The normal group is remarkable reserved and it appears, they all fall on the reverse extreme of the personality factor-A as possessed by the blind population. It confirms that they have reserved personality configuration.

Table 4.1 Personality factor - A: Reserve Vs Out going

Sl.	*Group*	*Boys*		*Girls*		*Boys+Girls*		*t/CRgd*	*CR*
		m	*S.D.*	*m*	*S.D.*	*m*	*S.D.*		
1.	Blind children	7.10	2.31	6.04	2.64	6.60	2.20	2.46	4.65**
2.	Normal children	4.24	1.24	4.01	1.18	5.25	1.96	2.30	
3.	Congenitally blind children	7.26	1.79	4.46	2.18	5.86	2.44	5.55**	3.30**
4.	Adventitiously blind children	7.10	1.62	7.62	2.06	7.28	1.76	5.36**	

** P< 0.01

When these groups are compared in relation to gender discrimination, it can be referred that the group i.e. BB and BG; NB and NG are found non-significant in relation to the personality factor-A. It further confirms that these groups are homogenous in their intra-group gender discrimination but followed the similar trend as mentioned above.

Only the last CR value (3.30) it found significant at 0.01 level. Mean sten values of adventitiously blind girls (ABG) and adventitiously blind boys and girls are showing upward trends on this personality factor but remaining group of congenitally blind girls (BG) and congenitally blind boys and girls have judicious mixture of reserved vs out going characteristics. CBB and ABB groups are comparatively homogeneous and superior on this personality factor. Significant gender discrimination presents high fluctuations in CBB and CBG groups which denote vividly that the girls (CBG) are extremely reserved nature, while the boys (CBB) sporting extremely outgoing personality factor. In case of ABB; ABG groups the minor variation and upward significant trend indicate outgoing attitudes with little dominance of the ABB group.

Table 4.2 Personality factor - B: Dull Vs Bright

Sl.	*Group*	*Boys*		*Girls*		*Boys+Girls*		*C Rgd*	*CR*
		m	*σ*	*m*	*σ*	*m*	*σ*		
1.	Blind children	3.94	1.57	4.28	1.71	4.11	2.77	1.03	1.10
2.	Normal children	3.56	1.30	3.98	1.44	3.77	1.36	1.61	
3.	Congenitally blind children	3.78	1.64	4.38	1.77	4.08	1.73	6.12**	0.18
4.	Adventitiously blind children	4.10	1.44	4.18	1.76	4.14	1.55	0.88**	

**P < 0.01

The calculated CR values on the Personality factor-B among the BB, BG, NB, NG; BBG, NBG (Blind boys and girls and normal boys and girls) groups are found 1.03, 1.61 and 1.10 respectively. The mean sten scores of the various group confirm that all the groups are almost homogeneous and remarkably characterised by the qualities of less intelligence.

The CRgd values representing gender discrimination are not found significant at any level, it shows that both the group are homogeneous and represent the less intelligent group of children without any cognitive distinction. The gender discrimination representing significant distinction in the case of CBB and CBB and CBG adhere to the group of less intelligent inmates. However the CBB group is severely suffered with a heavy loss on the other hand the ABB and ABG group do not express any sort of gender discrimination. They also belong to the group of poor intelligent inmates without sex biases.

The CR values among the blind and normal groups on personality factor is 1.08. This value is found not significant even at the 0.05 level. The mean values of blind and non-impaired group (4.48, 4.22) are fall down on the reverse extreme of the above personality factor. It reflects that the girls of both group are affected by feeling, hence represent emotional instability in their personality make-up. Although the BB, NB and BBG, NBG groups are homogeneous on this personality factor and they represent average emotionality in their affective make up.

Amongst boys and girls of both the group. The CR values on the personality factor-C are: 3.02 and 7.60 respectively which are found significant at 0.01 level. These values indicate that BB, BG, NB, NG groups have significant intra group differences. Further, it can be said that boys of both the groups have better build of their ego-strength than the girls while the BBG & NGB groups are combinedly marked by the factor of less stable emotionality.

Table 4.3 Personality factor - C: Affected by feeling Vs Emotionally Stable

Sl.	*Group*	*Boys*		*Girls*		*Boys+Girls*		*t/CRgd*	*CR*
		m	*o*	*m*	*o*	*m*	*o*		
1.	Blind children	5.54	1.92	4.48	1.67	4.97	1.82	3.02**	7.60**
2.	Normal children	6.12	1.12	4.42	1.22	5.52	2.27	1.08	
3.	Congenitally blind children	5.39	1.45	8.90	1.47	4.76	2.08	8.76	1.35
4.	Adventitiously blind children	5.38	2.14	4.82	1.45	5.20	1.00	4.33**	

** P < 0.01

The Table 4.3 also reveals that cogenital girls are emotionally less table and affected by feeling. Although CBB, ABB, ABG, CBBG, ABBG groups are homogeneous and they represent average qualities of this factor in their personality configuration.

The 't' values of boys and girls of CB and AB groups are found significant at 0.01 level. Mean values of both the groups indicate that girls are emotionally less stable than the boys.

Table 4.4 Personality factor - E: Humble Vs Assertive

Sl.	*Group*	*Boys*		*Girls*		*Boys+Girls*		*t/CRgd*	*CR*
		m	*o*	*m*	*o*	*m*	*o*		
1.	Blind children	6.46	1.44	6.48	8.26	6.03	1.89	0.05	1.89
2.	Normal children	6.94	1.18	7.44	1.93	5.81	1.72	1.16	
3.	Congenitally blind children	6.58	1.19	5.02	2.02	5.80	1.82	9.75**	2.59**
4.	Adventitiously blind children	6.34	1.64	7.18	2.02	6.76	1.95	7.63**	

**P <0.01

The calculated CR values on the personality Factor-E between blind and normal group is 1.89. Mean sten score of NG group (7.44) indicates that normal girls are assertive and independent in nature while the remaining groups are almost homogeneous. No gender discrimination exists among the groups as the CRgd values are not found significant even at the 0.05 level. However the mean sten scores of both the groups indicate that they all exhibit outwardly trends in their personality makeup toward assertiveness.

The scrutiny of the above table reveals that all the (CB & AB) groups under consideration differ significantly on this factor all 't' and CR values are found significant at 0.05 level. Mean values among the group i.e. CBB, ABG and ABBG exhibit assertive and independent trend in their personality, while the ABB, ABG and CBBG are having mixed personality trends in relation to Humble Vs Assertive..

When CB & AB are compared in relation to gender, it can be indicate that both the groups i.e. CBB, CBG and ABB, ABG are found significant at the 0.01 level. Hence, it confirms that CBB and ABG groups have superior trends in their personality. Congenital girls have calibrated this factor on average level but ABB group has excellent assertive trends.

A Scrutiny of the above table reveals that none of the five

groups under consideration differ significantly on this factor, it reflects that the groups do not have heterogeneity in relation to impairment and gender discrimination when these groups are compared on this personality factor. Moreover the trend inclined towards Happy-Go-lucky nature of all blind inmates and normal children as observed through mean sten scores, blind boys and girls excel on this factor than their counter parts.

Table 4.5 Personality factor - F: Sober Vs Happy-Go-Lucky

Sl.	*Group*	*Boys*		*Girls*		*Boys+Girls*		*t/CRgd*	*CR*
		m	*o*	*m*	*o*	*m*	*o*		
1.	Blind children	5.96	1.68	5.64	1.97	5.80	1.84	0.94	1.23
2.	Normal children	5.30	1.84	5.56	1.62	5.48	1.79	0.74	
3.	Congenitally blind children	6.38	1.96	4.36	1.80	5.66	2.07	12.68**	0.59
4.	Adventitiously blind children	5.82	1.58	6.34	1.85	5.88	1.75	5.30**	

** P < 0.01

Mean value of CBG group is having reverse trend and remaining all groups are homogeneous and show mixed personality configuration. The t value representing gender discrimination among the CB and AB groups are 12.68 and 5.30 in relation to the Personality Factor-F. The CBB group represents happy-go- lucky attitude in their personality development but the CBG group is extremely sober and having many inhibitions as compared on the basis of piling of scores on this factor. In case of ABB and ABG groups a reverse trend has been visualised as girls dominated the superior show by expressing happy-go-lucky mood in comparison than their counter parts.

Only the CR value (4.04) has been found significant at 0.01 level. It represents that the superior conscientious trend is existed in BBG and NBG group. But BBG group is out standingly superior in relation to it (mean sten, 7.48). The CR value (4.74 show significant differences between BB and BG groups. Mean sten score (7.32) of BG group exhibits that the girls are more conscientious in nature than their counterparts. Moreover the BB group adheres to the factor of expedient. In NI group the boys and girls are comparatively superior and almost homogeneous on this factor with inclination towards conscientiousness.

Table 4.6 Personality Factor - G: Expedient Vs Conscientious.

Sl.	*Group*	*Boys*		*Girls*		*Boys+Girls*		*t/CRgd*	*CR*
		m	*σ*	*m*	*σ*	*m*	*σ*		
1.	Blind children	5.58	1.61	7.32	2.04	7.48	1.78	4.74**	
2.	Normal children	6.14	1.74	6.80	1.67	6.47	1.70	1.94	4.04**
3.	Congenitally blind children	6.98	1.58	7.02	2.26	7.00	1.95	0.36	
4.	Adventitiously blind children	7.86	1.67	7.70	1.77	7.74	1.60	1.60	2.11

**P < 0.01

It is evident from the table 4.6 that there is no significant difference between congenital and adventitious blind children. The mean sten scores of these group indicate that ABB and ABG are found distinctly superior in relation to the factor conscientiousness. Gender discrimination does not has any influence on the groups separately.

The keen observation of table 4.7 shows that the computed CR values 8.05 is found significant at 0.01 level. The mean value of sten score (7.73) in case of normal children represents upward trend on the venturesome. The NB and BG groups exhibit the factor of thretia and shyness. The BB, NG; BBG groups are having mixed personality make up in relation to shyness Vs venturesome as represented by mean sten scores only 't' value between the groups of CBB and ABB is found not significant which represent that both group are homogeneous on the personality factor venturesome. Mean values of various groups indicate that girls of both groups exhibit the quality of shyness while the other groups show judicious mixture of this personality factor.

Table 4.7 Personality factor - H: Shy Vs Venturesome

Sl.	*Group*	*Boys*		*Girls*		*Boys+Girls*		*CRgd*	*CR*
		m	σ	m	σ	m	σ		
1.	Blind children	5.70	2.20	4.20	1.81	6.04	1.21	8.05**	
2.	Normal children	4.47	1.74	5.42	1.67	7.73	1.69	2.87**	
3.	Congenitally blind children	6.14	2.46	4.18	1.91	5.16	5.70	25.53**	
4.	Adventitiously blind children	5.26	1.81	4.26	1.76	5.52	1.90	5.36**	0.42

** P < 0.01

When these groups are compared in relation to gender discrimination, it can be referred that both the group i.e. BB, BG and NB, NG dragged towards the lower sten score which represent the personality factor of shyness in spite of existing significant gender discrimination. However more peculiar observation is that a reverse trend appears as the groups BB, NG are almost superior as they are trying to ushered towards the factor venturesome while the groups BG, NG are falling below this norm and strictly adhere to the factor of shyness in their personality makeup. It confirms that the BB and NG groups have calibrated this factor on average level but BG and NB groups are characterised by the quality of shyness. Gender discrimination of CB and AB groups indicate that the girls of both groups are characterized by the quality of shyness but boys of these groups have calibrated this factor on average level.

Only the CR values 9.89 is found significant at 0.01 level . It indicates differences among the groups. The mean sten scores of NG and NBG (5.92, 6.66) indicate a judicious mixture of Personality factor-I but remaining groups BB, BG, NB, NBG groups are exhibiting outward superiority in relation to the factor of Tender-mindedness, the above table also reveals that the computed CR values of congenitally blind and normal children is found 2.47 respectively. This value is significant at 0.01 and 0.05 level. Mean stenine scores the other groups are also following the similar congruence in their personality.

Table 4.8 Personality Factor - I: Tough Minded Vs Tender Minded

Sl.	Group	*Boys*		*Girls*		*Boys+Girls*		*t/CRgd*	*CR*
		m	*o*	*m*	*o*	*m*	*o*		
1.	Blind children	7.68	1.91	7.20	2.01	7.55	1.99	1.26	
2.	Normal children	7.48	1.92	5.92	2.27	6.06	2.20	3.90	9.89**
3.	Congenitally blind children	8.06	2.08	7.70	1.94	7.92	1.87	25.55**	
4.	Adventitiously blind children	7.34	1.84	6.62	1.97	6.98	1.92	5.36**	2.47*

** P < 0.01
* P < 0.05

Gender discrimination analysis show that the CR value among the normal boys and girls is found significant at 0.01 level. Mean sten values in both groups (Blind and NI) indicate that the normal children to net clear-cut placement on this trend while the remaining groups adhere to tender minded personality. When CB and AB groups are compared in relation to gender discrimination. It can be referred that both of groups CBB, CBG, ABB, ABG are found significant at the 0.01 level. It further confirms that boys are extremely excelled but the girls also followed the trend in relation to tender mindedness with slow pace.

The table 4.9 reveals that the blind and normal groups are found almost similar in relation to the personality factor-L. When interpretation can be carried out on the basis of mean sten scores it can be said that all the group have their indication towards below average level. Hence they all characterised by trusting trends in their personality. Mean values (3.54; 5.22) of their group reveals that CBG group exhibits the trusting qualities in their personality, the remaining of groups CB and AB are characterised by the suspicious nature. In respect to gender discrimination, it can be said that both groups have significant differences and exhibiting the qualities of trust worthiness. Similar trends have been existed in relation to gender discrimination as expressed by CRgd and mean sten values.

Table 4.9 Personality Factor - L: Trusting Vs Suspicious

Sl.	*Group*	*Boys*		*Girls*		*Boys+Girls*		*t/CRgd*	*CR*
		m	*o*	*m*	*o*	*m*	*o*		
1.	Blind children	4.76	2.12	4.08	2.11	4.37	2.29	0.43	
2.	Normal children	4.62	1.92	4.90	2.90	4.86	2.53	0.58	0.94
3.	Congenitally blind children	4.70	2.68	3.54	3.95	4.12	2.46	7.75**	
4.	Adventitiously blind children	4.42	2.29	5.22	1.86	4.98	2.21	3.90**	1.87

**P <0.01

Table 4.10 Personality Factor - M: Practical Vs Imagination

Sl.	*Group*	*Boys*		*Girls*		*Boys+Girls*		*t/CRgd*	*CR*
		m	*s.d*	*m*	*s.d*	*m*	*s.d*		
1.	Blind children	7.68	2.14	6.62	2.04	7.26	1.66	2.38**	
2.	Normal children	7.26	1.63	7.20	1.73	7.23	1.68	0.18	0.13
3.	Congenitally blind children	7.70	2.17	7.46	2.63	7.58	2.21	2.00**	
4.	Adventitiously blind children	7.86	2.16	5.94	1.74	6.06	4.26	17.45**	2.24

** P < 0.01

The above table reveals that blind and NI groups a real most homogenous in relation to factor-M. Hence both groups show superiority on this factor when judged on the basis of mean sten scores. It represent imaginative qualities in their personality makeup. The girls of CB and AB group differentiate on this factor. ABG group is calibrated the average quality and adhere to the norm of practicality in their routine life. It further indicate that CBB, ABB, CBG, CBBG, ABBG groups are more imaginative than their counter parts.

In respect to gender discrimination, it can be said that blind boys are more imaginative than the girls, while the NB, NG groups are almost homogeneous and forms the group of highly imaginative children. The 't' values of boys and girls in CB and AB group are found 2.00 and 17.47 respectively. The 't' value of adventitious group is found significant at 0.01 level. Mean score of this group indicates that the girls are calibrated to average quality on this factor, while the boys are marked by the viewed imagination in their personality configuration.

Table 4.11 Personality Factor - N: Forthright Vs Shrewd

Sl.	*Group*	*Boys*		*Girls*		*Boys+Girls*		*t/CRgd*	*CR*
		m	*s.d*	*m*	*s.d*	*m*	*s.d*		
1.	Blind children	7.18	6.62	5.40	1.26	6.10	1.05	2.07	
2.	Normal children	7.16	2.01	6.70	1.94	6.26	2.00	1.17	3.30**
3.	Congenitally blind children	7.80	1.20	6.22	1.48	6.76	1.42	16.56**	
4.	Adventitiously blind children	7.06	1.50	7.02	2.67	7.00	1.85	10.32 **	0.73

** P <0.01

It is evident from the table 4.11 that the CR value between the groups blind and normal children are found significant at 0.01 level. The mean scores in these groups indicate that the normal group of children has prominent shrewd qualities in comparison to the blind group. Mean score of this group show that girls of congenital blind are characterized by the average level on the personality factor-N, while the remaining groups are homogeneous and remarkably shrewd personality.

There exists no gender discrimination in relation to factor-N between blind and NI groups. The 't' values of boys and girls of CB and AB on the personality factor-N are 16.56 and 0.32 respectively. Out of these the 't' value of congenital group is found significant at the 0.01 level. Mean score of this group indicates that CBG group is calibrated mixed personality on this factor, while the ABG group is dominated by the factor of shrewdness and self centredness.

Table 4.12 Personality Factor - O: Placid Vs Apprehensive

Sl.	*Group*	*Boys*		*Girls*		*Boys+Girls*		*t/CRgd*	*CR*
		m	*o*	*m*	*o*	*m*	*o*		
1.	Blind children	6.62	1.91	6.54	1.91	6.38	1.89	0.89	
2.	Normal children	7.06	1.94	6.12	1.51	6.59	1.97	2.85**	0.77
3.	Congenitally blind children	5.94	1.96	7.42	1.94	6.76	2.16	16.56**	
4.	Adventitiously blind children	7.34	1.84	6.08	1.56	6.06	1.44	0.32	1.94

** P < 0.01

The above table reveals that there is no significant difference between blind and non - impaired children. The mean sten scores support the evidence that NB group is highly inclined towards the guilt-proneness than the BB. It can be observed from the above table that the ABB and CBG groups are having superior trend in relation to apprehensiveness. The remaining groups are having mixed personality makeup in relation to placid Vs apprehensive. Moreover the CBB group from the placid personality.

When these groups are compared in relation to gender discrimination, it can be inferred that boys and girls of congenital groups are found significant at 0.01 level. Mean scores of CBG and ABB groups indicate extremely dominance to apprehensive qualities in their personality structure. Similarly significant CRgd value (2.85) existed in NI group represents the out standing superior apprehensive factor in case of boys (NB).

It is evident from the above table that there exists no significant differences among the blind and normal group on factor- Q1. Mean values of each group indicate that these groups are almost similar and have judiciously balanced trends in their personality makeup on this factor (conservative Vs Experimenting). On other hand mean scores of CB and AB group indicate that CBB and ABB are having some differences but scores of both group are piled upon average level. While the other groups are homogeneous on this factor and having mixed personality makeup on the conservative Vs experimenting.

Table 4.13 Personality Factor - Q1: Conservative Vs Experimenting

Sl.	*Group*	*Boys*		*Girls*		*Boys+Girls*		*t/CRgd*	*CR*
		m	*o*	*m*	*o*	*m*	*o*		
1.	Blind children	5.46	1.60	4.76	5.13	1.94	2.38	2.38**	0.32
2.	Normal children	5.08	1.72	5.00	2.25	5.04	1.99	1.89	
3.	Congenitally blind children	5.66	1.57	4.86	2.04	5.26	1.86	7.3**	0.20
4.	Adventitiously visually impaired children	5.34	1.70	4.66	2.25	5.18	2.14	5.97**	

**P <0.01

The CR values of BB and BG is significant at the 0.01 level. Further the mean values (3.38) of this group confirms that the blind girls are exclusively dependent in nature than the BB group, Non-impaired boys and girls have no significant difference in relation to factor-Q3. They depict the development trends from group dependence to self sufficiency. The 't' values representing the gender discrimination among congenital and adventitious group on this factor are 7.3 and 5.91 respectively. Mean values of both groups indicates that the girls of both groups fall on reverse trend of the personality factor and boys of these groups exhibit average level of conservative Vs experimenting factor.

The mean score of Blind group indicates that the blind children are dependent, while the other group of Non impaired children are appeared to be self sufficient nature. The mean score of CBG fall on reverse side of the group dependents. While the other groups are homogeneous on this factor and exhibited the mixed personality make up in relation to group dependent Vs self sufficient.

Table 4.14 Personality Factor - Q2: Group Dependent Vs Self Sufficient

Sl.	*Group*	*Boys*		*Girls*		*Boys+Girls*		*t/CRgd*	*CR*
		m	*σ*	*m*	*σ*	*m*	*σ*		
1.	Blind children	6.00	1.76	4.62	1.87	5.38	1.89	3.83**	0.36
2.	Normal children	5.57	1.98	5.30	1.49	5.47	1.69	0.58	
3.	Congenitally blind children	5.66	1.86	4.42	1.65	5.04	1.88	12.27**	1.32
4.	Adventitiously blind children	6.26	1.61	4.82	2.01	5.54	1.96	13.71**	

** P < 0.01

In respect to gender discrimination, it confirms that the blind girls group is exclusively dependent in nature than the blind boys group. Non-impaired boys and girls have no significant difference in relation to factor- Q3. They depict two development trends from group dependence to self- sufficiency. Congenital and adventitious groups have significant difference on this factor in respect to gender discrimination. Girls of CB and AB group show high dependence qualities than their counterparts.

The table 4.15 explains that Mean score of the boys of blind & NI groups (8.28 and 7.26) reveal that blind boys are marked by better emotional control. The normal boys group also reveals favourable control, while the remaining group i.e. BG, NG, BBG, NBG are expressing outwardly superior trends in their personality makeup representing controlled personality. Mean scores of congenital and adventitious groups show that adventitiously blind children are superior on this factor and marked by the factor better emotionality, while the remaining groups are having outwardly trend in their personality make up.

Table 4.15 Personality Factor-Q3: Undisciplined Self-Conflict Vs Controlled

Sl.	*Group*	*Boys*		*Girls*		*Boys+Girls*		*CRgd*	*CR*
		m	*σ*	*m*	*σ*	*m*	*σ*		
1.	Blind children	8.28	1.87	7.18	10.19	7.15	2.18	0.83	1.31
2.	Normal children	7.26	2.32	8.97	2.09	7.57	2.38	4.07**	
3.	Congenitally blind children	7.70	2.29	6.28	2.31	6.88	2.44	11.00**	3.58**
4.	Adventitiously blind children	8.50	1.83	8.38	2.07	8.42	1.92	1.07	

** P < 0.01

The CR value (4.07) in NI group is found significant at 0.01 level. The mean sten value of this group (7.26, 8.97) indicates that normal girls (NG) are more superior on this factor. Hence it can be interpreted that the NG group is highly emotionally controlled than boys of this group. The t value of boys and girls of congenital and adventitious group are 11.00 and 1.07 respectively. The 't' value of congenital group is found significant at the 0.01 level. Mean value of this group indicates that girls are calibrated judicious mixture of above personality factor and other group are having higher trend on the factor-Q3.

The table 4.16 reveals that the CR values between the blind and normal children indicates that the significant differences between Blind and NI groups in relation to PF-Q4. The mean sten value of NG group shows Relaxed trends in their personality. While the other groups are homogeneous on this factor and having mired personality makeup in relation to relaxed Vs Tense as evident from the mean scores (5.62, 6.28, 6.01 and 5.34). The 't' values of congenitally and adventitiously visually are found significant at the 0.05 level. Mean scores in these groups indicate that congenital girls are extremely Relaxed while the adventitiously blind girls groups is comparatively tense.

Table 4.16 Personality factor - Q4: Relaxed Vs Tense

Sl.	Group	Boys		Girls		Boys+Girls		CRgd	CR
		m	*σ*	*m*	*σ*	*m*	*σ*		
1.	Blind children	5.62	1.95	6.01	2.00	6.44	1.98	2.06	3.79**
2.	Normal children	6.28	2.12	4.90	1.59	5.34	2.08	3.72**	
3.	Congenitally blind children	5.74	1.68	4.50	1.74	5.42	1.60	13.77**	0.38
4.	Adventitiously blind children	5.90	2.05	5.14	2.07	5.56	2.12	0.74	

** P < 0.01

When blind and NI groups are compared in relation to gender discrimination. It can be said that boys and girls of normal group are significantly differ from each other. Further it can be said that normal girls are possessing relaxed trends in their personality makeup than their counterparts. Blind boys and girls groups are homogeneous on this factor Q-4. When CB and AB groups compared in relation to gender discrimination, it can be said that congenital group is found significant at the 0.01 level. Mean value indicates that CBG groups is more relaxed then the boys. Adventitious boys and girls are homogeneous on this personality factor-Q4.

OVERVIEW OF THE CHAPTER

In this chapter the personality factors blind children and normal children, congenitally blind children and adventitiously blind Children, gender discrimination in the personality make up of various groups are presented and analysed. The method used for analysing the data are CR and t test. The next chapter draws upon the creative potential of blind and normal children.

5

CREATIVE POTENTIAL OF BLIND AND NORMAL CHILDREN

In this chapter the creative potential of blind and normal children, congenitally and adventitiously blind children, gender discrimination in the creative potential of various groups are presented and analysed. The method used for establishing the differences are CR and t test. The author has analysed the result in fallowing table. It leads to smoother extraction of creative potential and its constituents i.e. fluency, flexibility and originality.

The table 5.1 reveals that the CR value of blind and normal children are found not significant at any level. Mean scores of both the groups show that normal groups have better fluency in their creative ability. While the blind and non impaired girls are homogeneous and exhibiting poor fluency. The table 5.1 reveals that congenital blind and adventitious blind children have no significant difference on this dimension of creativity. Boys of congenital and adventitious group and girls of both groups are having significant differences. Mean values of these group indicate that the group of congenitally visually impaired children and adventitiously blind children (ABBG) are homogeneous on this constituent i.e. fluency.

Table 5.1 Comparison of Fluency

Sl.	*Group*	*Boys*		*Girls*		*Boys+Girls*		*CR/tgd*	*CR*
		m	*o*	*m*	*o*	*m*	*o*		
1.	Blind children	32.12	4.52	29.12	4.36	32.84	4.62	3.40**	
2.	Normal children	36.02	4.89	31.27	3.01	32.12	4.52	5.92**	0.01
3.	Congenitally blind children	28.96	4.73	28.04	4.13	29.12	4.83	3.08**	
4.	Adventitiously blind children	29.88	4.34	28.76	4.20	29.72	4.39	4.66**	0.65

** P< 0.01

To evaluate the gender discrimination between the groups of blind and normal is found significant at 0.01 level. The mean scores indicate that boys are extremely superior in the groups of blind children and normal children in relation to the fluency constituents of creative potential. The t value among the congenital boys and girls and adventitious boys and girls groups are found significant at 0.01 level. It indicates that the boys of both groups are outstandingly superior in comparison than their counterparts. Although all the groups have only slight fluctuations on fluency scores.

Table 5.2 Comparison of Flexibility

Sl.	*Group*	*Boys*		*Girls*		*Boys+Girls*		*CR/tgd*	*CR*
		m	*o*	*m*	*o*	*m*	*o*		
1.	Blind children	27.76	4.43	25.48	4.40	26.62	2.46	-2.45**	
2.	Normal children	28.98	4.01	26.02	4.28	20.12	4.83	3.60**	4.62**
3.	Congenitally blind children	27.88	4.99	23.24	3.62	25.12	4.89	16.92**	
4.	Adventitiously blind children	27.64	5.20	27.72	5.87	28.16	4.44	0.51	3.26**

** P < 0.01

The computed CR values on flexibility among the blind and normal children are found significant at 0.01 level. The mean score of both groups indicate that normal children are outstandingly superior on flexibility scores of creative potential than their counterparts. It further confirms that vision plays on important role to produce a great variety of idea which nourishes the flexibility scores between congenitally blind and adventitiously blind children is found significant at 0.01 level. This significant difference show that adventitiously blind children exhibit superior flexibility in comparison to the congenitally impaired group.

However, the CR values calculated for gender discrimination indicate that the boys and girls of blind and normal groups are having some differences on this creativity constituent i.e. flexibility. Mean scores of both the groups indicate that boys are far better on flexibility than their counter parts. The t values of boys and girls among the CB and AB groups are 16.92 and 0.51 respectively. The 't' value of CBB, CBG are significant. Mean scores of this group show that the congenitally blind boys are superior on flexibility than the girls.

Table 5.3 Comparison of Originality

Sl.	*Group*	*Boys*		*Girls*		*Boys+Girls*		*CR/tgd*	*CR*
		m	*o*	*m*	*o*	*m*	*o*		
1.	Blind children	28.06	4.58	18.88	4.58	18.42	2.42	12.29**	
2.	Normal children	30.72	4.79	24.88	3.58	28.02	4.48	6.94**	19.20**
3.	Congenitally blind children	18.92	5.00	12.68	5.00	15.40	5.90	22.18**	
4.	Adventitiously blind children	18.84	4.99	15.24	3.45	18.08	4.76	15.00**	2.85**

** P < 0.01

It is evident from the above table that CR values of blind and NI groups are found significant at 0.01 level. The mean values of all the three groups of normal category indicate that NB, NG, NBG are excelled in relation to originality scores of creative potential. However, the BB group is extremely superior in relation to it, the BG and BBG are homogeneous in relation to originality when the whole group is combined and compared with in the group. Hence it can be inferred that the blind children group as a whole adheres to the norm of below average originality in comparison to normal children. But over-all the girls are found in very poor condition of originality scores when compared to their counterparts. Mean values of both the group CB children and AB children indicate that adventitiously blind children are superior than that of congenitally blind children. Boys of both group CB and AB are homogeneous on this creative ability.

The CR values noting gender discrimination are found significant at 0.01 level. Both values indicate that the boys of blind and normal groups are remarkably superior on the originality scores of creativity. It further confirms that boys excel in generating new ideas under all the academic and non-academic perspective.

Table 5.4 Comparison of Creative Potential

Sl.	*Group*	*Boys*		*Girls*		*Boys+Girls*		*CR/tgd*	*CR*
		m	*o*	*m*	*o*	*m*	*o*		
1.	Blind children	73.30	10.50	63.65	9.60	68.60	11.66	22.28**	2.85**
2.	Normal children	75.10	14.20	65.20	9.71	70.90	9.42	15.00**	
3.	Congenitally blind children	70.90	14.90	58.80	11.90	64.20	14.76	6.20**	20.85**
4.	Adventitiously blind children	74.80	7.49	65.00	8.85	63.90	10.39	0.18	

** P < 0.01

The calculated CR values on creative potential among blind and normal children are found significant at 0.01 level. Mean scores show that non impaired children are having out standingly superior creative potentialities than their counterparts. The table 5.4 reflect that adventitiously impaired group is superior on the creative potential.

When comparisons are made among the group BB, BG and NB, NG separately to make gender discrimination analysis prove it at 0.01 level. In both groups the boys exalt in overall creativity than their counterparts. It also observed that the non impaired boys are for better in their creative potential than the blind children. In both the group (Blind & NI) the girls suffered a heavy loss in their creativity. The t values of boys and girls of CB and AB groups are found significant at 0.01 level. Mean scores indicate that the boys are superior in relation to creative potential than their counter parts.

OVERVIEW OF THE CHAPTER

In this chapter, the interpretation of data on Creative potential of blind children and normal children, congenitally blind children and adventitiously blind children are presented. The interpretation of creative potential are based on various dimension of creativity like Fluency, Flexibility and Originality.

6

INTERPRETATION BASED ON PERSONALITY PROFILES: BLIND AND NORMAL CHILDREN

The in-depth scrutiny of the comparative personality profile (Fig. 6.1) vividly reveals that the blind group of children (BC) surpass the other group on the personality factors -A; E and G respectively. It denotes the clinical qualities like affectothymia, dominance, and better build of their super ego.

On the contrary the normal boys and girls (NBG) has the peculiar personality configuration as envisaged by the personality factors-H, I, N and Q4. It exhibits that the group possesses the qualities like- venturesome, premsia (sensitive and tender-mindedness), shrewdness marked by tension.

Further, both the groups (Blind and normal) are similar in relation to the personality factors- C, L, Q1 and Q2 respectively. As these groups concentrated their sten score with the average range, it can be said that they were swinging between the personality factors characterized by ego-strength; alaxia (trusting) to protension (suspiciousness); conservative to experimenting; and group adherence to self-sufficiency.

The last critical and visible trend is marked by the inter-group similarity. It has upward piling up of scores on the

FIG 6.1: A COMPARATIVE PERSONALITY PROFILE OF BLIND CHILDREN (BC) AND NORMAL CHILDREN (NC)

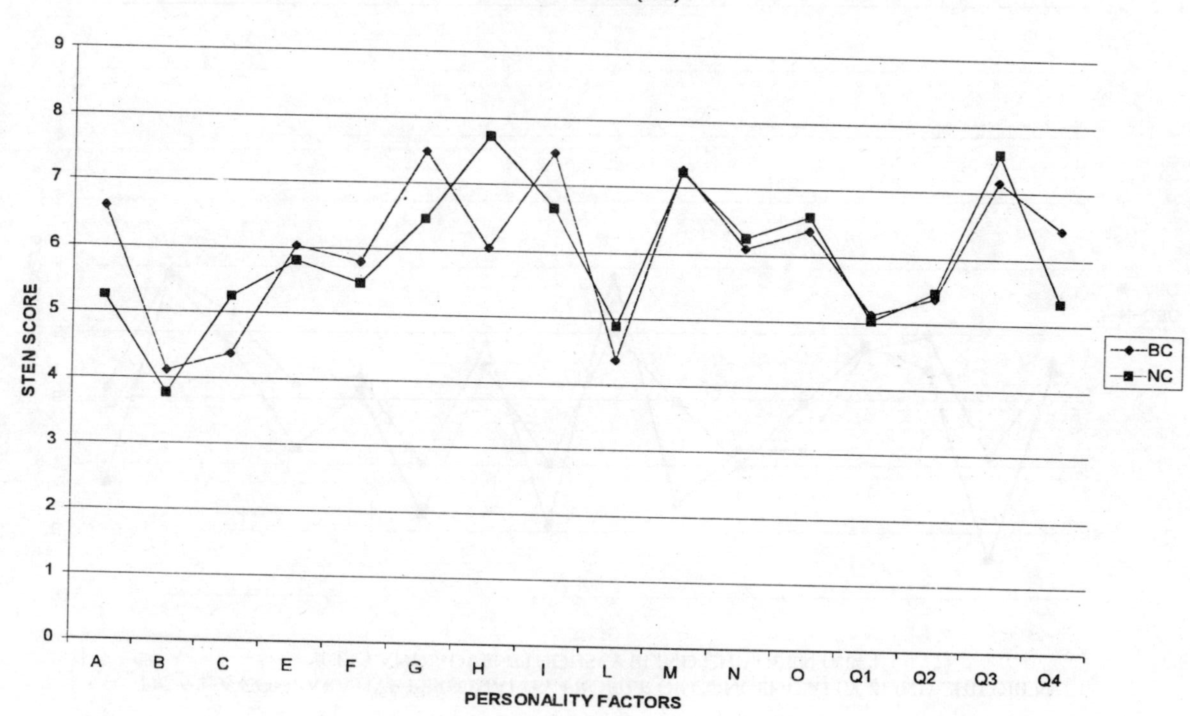

FIG 6.2: A COMPARATIVE PERSONALITY PROFILE OF CONGENITALLY BLIND CHILDREN (CBC) AND ADVENTITIOUSLY BLIND CHILDREN (ABC)

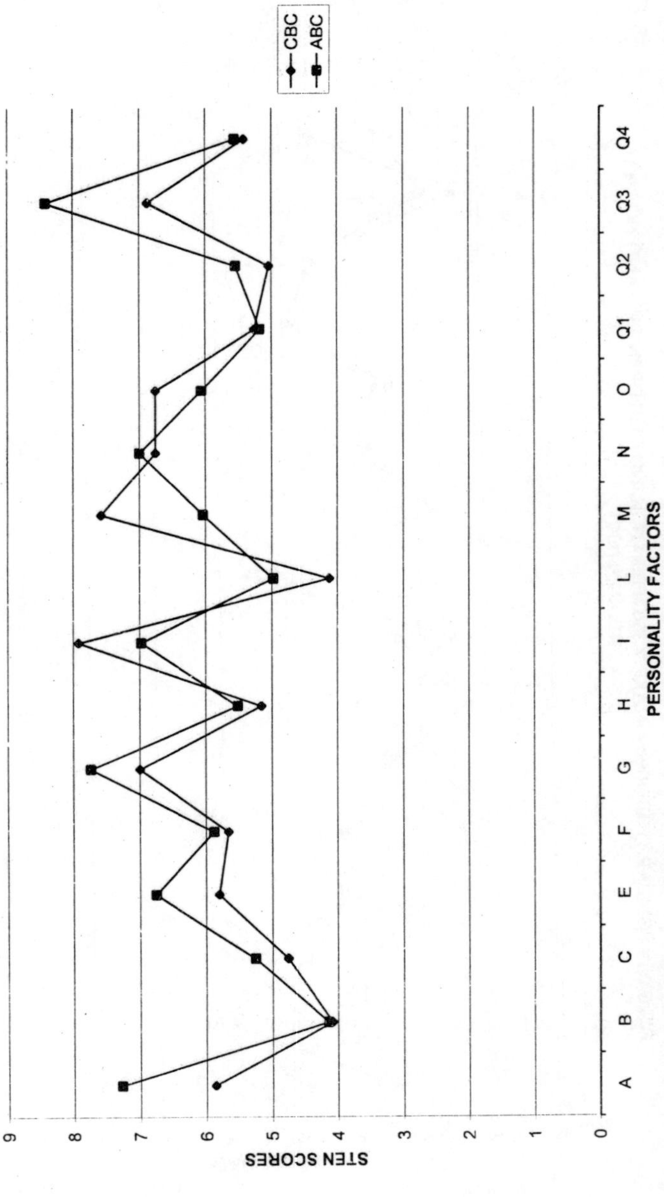

STEN SCORES

0 1 2 3 4 5 6 7 8 9

A B C E F G H I L M N O Q1 Q2 Q3 Q4

PERSONALITY FACTORS

CBC
ABC

personality factors- F, M, O and Q3 while the downward (below average) trend in relation to factor-B. It summarizes that both the groups (blind and Normal children) are characterized by the personality factors of happy-go-lucky; imaginative; apprehensive and controlled emotionally. The specific feature shown by the personality profile is that both the groups are represented by less intelligent and poor cognition personality factor (B).

2. CONGENITALLY BLIND (CB) AND ADVENTITIOUSLY BLIND (AB) CHILDREN

The personality profile (Fig 6.2) has revealed two prominent trends i.e. the high trend in the group AB of the personality factors- A; E; G; I and Q3 while the CB group spurts on the personality factors- M and O. Both the groups of blind children are homogeneous in relation to the factors-C; F; H; Q1; Q2 and Q4 respectively.

Thus the intra-group differences represent the group AB by the personality factors affectothymia; assertive attitude; conscientious; premsia; and better build of emotionality. On the other hand the CB group is marked by the imaginative and apprehensive personality configuration.

The existing commonalities in their personality profiles are normally developed ego-strength, lead a normal life (sober and happy-go-lucky) without showing timid behaviour. They are appeared to be stable without lying on the extreme ends of the personality factors like-introversion Vs extraversion (Q1), low anxiety Vs high anxiety (Q2); and subdueness Vs independence (Q4) respectively.

INTERPRETATION BASED ON PERSONALITY PRO FILES: GENDER DISCRIMINATION BLIND BOYS (BB) AND BLIND GIRLS (BG)

The profile (6.3) exhibits high trend of the Personality factors of A; I; M; N and Q3 in blind boys, while the blind girls represent only two factors on high trend i.e. I and Q3. The BB

FIG 6.3: A COMPARATIVE PERSONALITY PROFILE OF BLIND BOY (BB) AND BLIND GIRLS (BG)

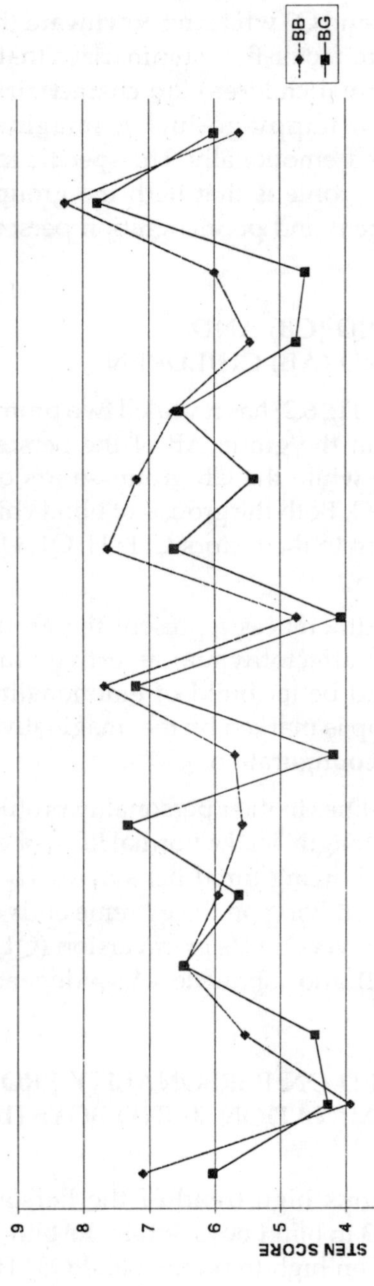

groups is having downward trend of personality factor-B. Similarly the BG group represents downward trend of personality factors- A; B; C; H; L and Q2 respectively.

Both of the groups (BB and BG) are similar in relation to Personality factors-E; F; G; O; Q1 and Q4. It can be said that they are swinging between the personality characteristics from low to higher trend. It can be referred that BB group is marked by Personality factors as Outgoing; Imaginative; Shrewd and Emotionally balance, while the BG are having Outgoing; Tender-minded and Emotionally balanced characteristics.

CONGENITALLY BLIND BOYS (CBB) AND CONGENITALLY BLIND GIRLS (CBG)

The Fig 6.4 show that the CBB group of children have marked superiority on the personality factors- A; E; F; G; H; I; M; N and Q3. Similarly, the CBG group has represented gender discrimination through the personality factors- G; I; M and O. Moreover, the common trend of personality factors has been witnessed by B, C, L, O, Q1 and Q4.

One more peculiar down ward trend can be analysed in case of CBG only in relation to the personality factors- A; B; C; F; H; L, Q1 Q2 and Q4 respectively. It reflects that this group has followed the preceding group with more prominence in relation to gender discrimination. The groups under consideration do not show any distinction in relation to Submissiveness Vs Dominance (E); Desurgency Vs Surgency, Placid Vs Experimenting; and Relaxed Vs Tense (Q4) respectively. They represent an average and similar trend in relation to these factors.

ADVENTITIOUSLY BLIND BOYS (ABB) AND ADVENTITIOUSLY BLIND GIRLS (ABG)

here the profile given in Fig 6.5 follows the similar trend of gender discrimination as in the groups BB and BG. Identically the Personality factors- A; M; N; and Q3 have the upward trend in the ABB group. It indicates that the ABB group is having

FIG 6.4 : A COMPARATIVE PERSONALITY PROFILE OF CONGENITALLY BLIND BOY (CBB) AND CONGENITALLY BLIND GIRLS (CBG)

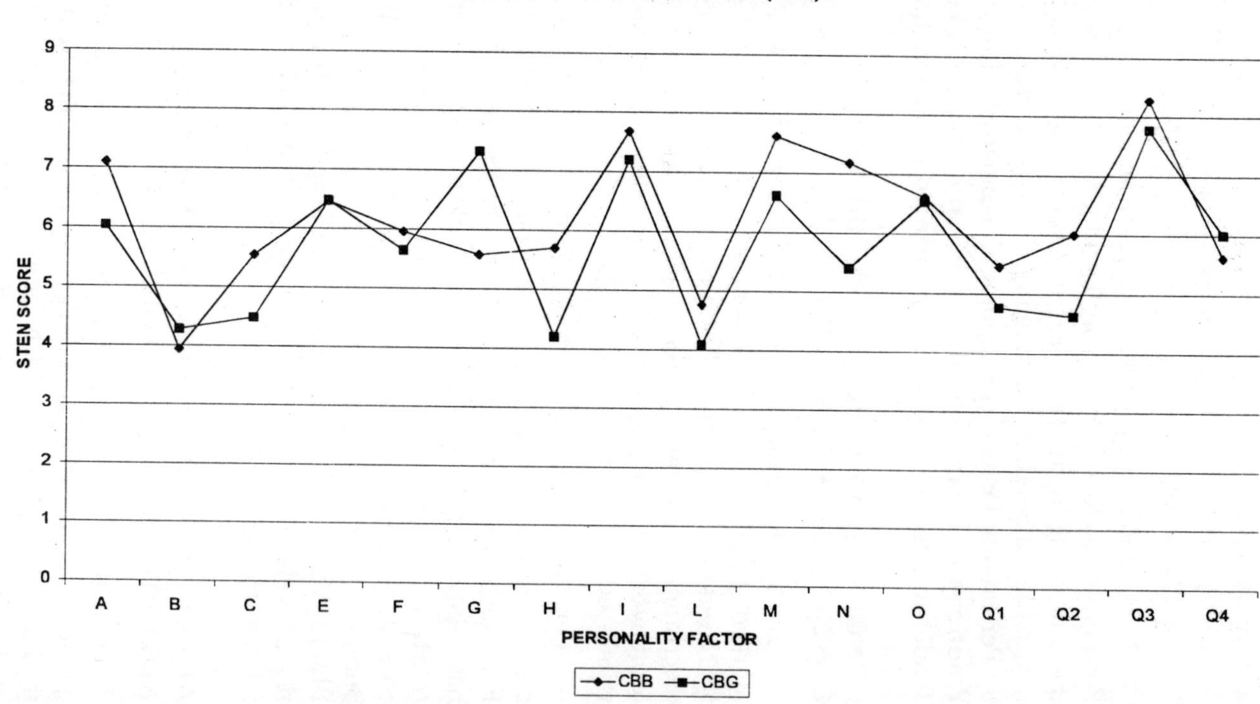

Fig 6.5: COMPARATIVE PERSONALITY PROFILE OF ADVENTITIOUSLY BLIND BOYS (ABB) AND ADVENTITIOUSLY BLIND GIRLS (ABG)

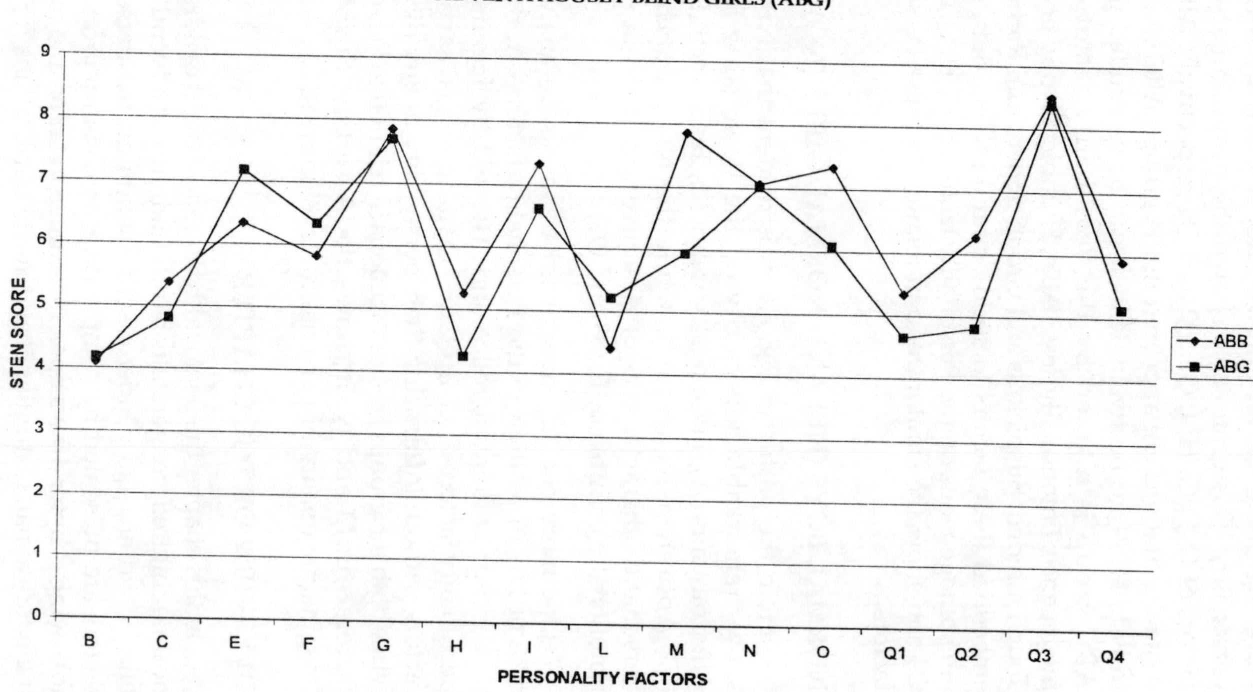

Outgoing, Imaginative, Shrewd and Emotionally controlled personality. This group also shown the common personality factors of C; E; G; H; I; Q1; Q2 and Q4 respectively. Although more fluctuations are appeared in the groups ABG in relation to F; L; M; N; respectively. Thus it can be concluded that the ABG group is marked by the Personality factors- Less intelligence; Emotionally; less stable; Humble; Happy-go-lucky; Tough minded; Suspicious and Group dependent. Rather they embedded these factors to socio-cultural milieu. Both groups are homogeneous on the Personality factors b; G; H; Q; Q3 and Q4 and show the similar trend in relation to these Personality factors.

NORMAL BOYS (NB) AND NORMAL GIRLS (NG)

From the profile in Fig. 6.6, it is evident that NB group shows remarkable superiority on the Personality factors- Affectothymia (A); Emotional stability (c); Tender-mindedness (T); Apprehensiveness (O), while the NG group has the Personality characteristics of Assertiveness; Tension ridden; Emotionally controlled (E, Q3 and Q4)

One more peculiar downward trend can be analysed in case of NG in relation to the Personality factors- A, B and C (Reserved, Less-intelligence and Affected by feeling). The personality factors- F; G; L; Q1 and Q2 are emerged as common factors without influencing their personality in any direction, while both the groups are homogenous in relation to Personality factors - E; M and N. It shows the Assertive; Suspicious; Imaginative quality of personality development.

OVERVIEW OF THE CHAPTER

In this chapter the personality factors of blind children and normal children, congenitally blind children and adventitiously blind children, and gender discrimination on the personality factors are presented by comparative personality profile. The following chapter draws upon these interpretation and outlines the educational, institutional and social implications for better

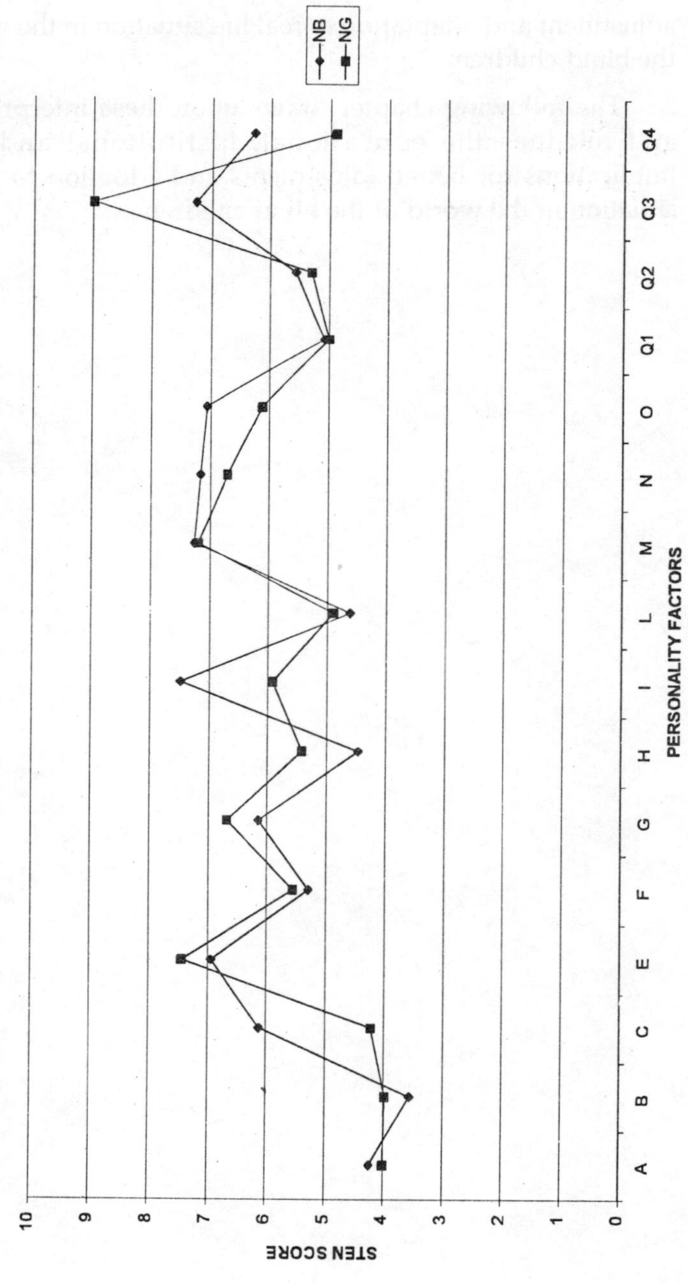

FIG 6.6: COMPARATIVE PERSONALITY PROFILE OF NORMAL BOYS (NB) AND NORMAL GIRLS (NG)

adjustment and adaptation to real life situation in the world of the blind children.

The following chapter draws upon these interpretations and outlines the educational, institutional and social implications for better adjustments and adoption to real life situation in the world of the blind children.

7

FINDINGS OF THE STUDY

In this chapter, an attempt has been made by the researcher to summarize major findings on the basis of preceding chapter to give a global glimpse of the present study.

PERSONALITY FACTORS OF BLIND AND NORMAL CHILDREN

The CR values between blind and normal groups are found significant on some personality factors. The table 7.1 reveals that seven out of sixteen Personality factors are found significant viz. A; E; G; H; I; N; and Q4. It can be said that blind children are Easy - going; Assertive; Tender-minded with Extroversive tendencies on the contrary the normal children have the peculiar personality factors like Sensitiveness, Tender- mindedness and Shrewdness.

Comparison of boys of blind and normal groups indicate that normal boys are having Reserve; Less intelligence, Thretia; and Alaxia Trait in their personality makeup. While the girls of both groups exhibited the balanced personality while the girls of both groups exhibited the balanced personality makeup in relation to Personality Factors-F; N; O and Q1. BG group represents the Reserve and Trusting nature of personality configuration.

Table 7.1: Determination and Comparison of Personality Factors among the groups

Sl.	*PF*	*Personality Factors*	*BC NC* 1	*CBC ABC* 2	*Explanation*
1.	A	Reserved Vs Outgoing	*	*	Blind children and AB children are easy-going while NC and CBC children are reserved and detached.
2.	B	Less Intelligence Vs More Intelligent	_	_	There exist no significant differences among the groups.
3.	C	Affected by Feeling Vs Emotionally stable	_	_	None of the groups have significant differences.
4.	E	Humble Vs Assertive	*	*	Blined and AB children are more assertive and independent. The CB and Normal children are marked by mixed personality on this factor.
5.	F	Sober Vs Happy-go-lucky	-	-	There exists no significant differences among the groups.
6.	G	Expedient Vs Conscien-entious	*	*	Blind children are outstandingly conscientious in comparison than the remaining groups.

Sl.	*PF*	*Personality Factors*	*BC NC 1*	*CBC ABC 2*	*Explanation*
7.	H	Shy Vs Venturesome	*	_	Normal children are eager to take new ventures because they are socially bold, uninhibited and spontaneous.
8.	I	Tough-minded Vs Tender-minded	*	*	Blind and CB groups of children are found extremely superior in relation to tender mindedness, while the other groups are also following the similar trend.
9.	L	Trusting Vs Imaginative	_	_	There exists no significant difference among the groups.
10.	M	Practical Vs Imaginative	_	*	CB groups in highly imaginative but other groups are having no significant differences.
11.	N	Forthright Vs Shrewd	*	-	Group of normal children has exhibited shrewdness while the remaining groups have favourable trend.
12.	O	Placid Vs Apprehensive	-	-	There exists no significant

Sl.	*PF*	*Personality Factors*	*BC NC* 1	*CBC ABC* 2	*Explanation*
					differences and they are marked by the personality configuration.
13.	Q1	Conservative Vs Experimenting	-	-	None of the group have significant differences and they are marked by the personality configuration.
14.	Q2	Group dependent Vs self sufficient	-	-	No significant differences among the groups are found.
15.	Q3	Undisciplined self conflict Vs Controlled	-	*	AB children are marked by better emotionally control, while the other groups also reveal favourable control.
16.	Q4	Relaxed Vs Tense	*	-	Normal children are found completely relaxed while the other groups are mild in reference to this personality factor.

* P< 0.05

CBC= congenitally Blind children NC = Normal children

ABC= Adventitiously Blind children

BC = Blind Children

CREATIVE POTENTIAL OF BLIND AND NORMAL CHILDREN

The Table 7.2 reveals that blind and non - impaired children are having significant difference in relation to creative potential and its components viz. Fluency; Flexibility; alongwith Originality.

Table 7.2: Determination and Comparison of Creative Potential among the groups

Sl.	*Constituents of Creative Potential*	**BC **NC*	**CB **AB*	*Explanations*
1.	Fluency	-	-	There exists no significant difference among the groups in relation to Fluency scores.
2.	Flexibility	**	**	Normal children , and Adventitiously blind children are outstandingly superior on Flexibility scores of creative potential than their counterparts.
3.	Originality	**	**	Normal children and adventitiously visually impaired children exalted superior in relation to originality scores of creative potential.
4.	Creative Potential	**	-	Non-impaired children have extremely superior creative potential whereas the intra-group comparison among the blind children revealed no difference.

**$P < 0.01$

**BC = Blind children

**CB = Congenitally blind

**NC = Normal Children **AB = Adventitiously Blind

The group of Blind children show poor creative potential, while the normal children have superior creative potentiality. Analysis of data further shows that normal children are more superior on the constituents of creative potential like-flexibility and originality.

When comparison has been made between blind and normal groups, the findings suggested that normal boys (NB) and normal girls (NG) are better in creative potential and also its constituents (Fluency, Flexibility, Originality). It indicates that vision plays an important role in the development of creative potential.

PERSONALITY FACTORS OF CONGENITALLY BLIND (CB) AND ADVENTITIOUSLY BLIND (AB) CHILDREN

Table 7.1 reveals that CB children are considerably differ in their personality makeup from adventitiously impaired children with respect to factors- A; E; G; I; M and Q3. The intra-group comparison referred that AB children are Out going; Independent; Tender-minded and showing Controlled behaviour. On the other hand congenitally impaired children are having imaginative and Apprehensive personality configuration.

Comparison of CBB and ABB on the Personality factors indicate that CBB group is being characterised by the personality factors-B; E; F; G; H; I; Q; Q1 and Q3 and Q3 respectively. Thus this group is marked by Less intelligent and Tender-mindedness but the ABB are more Assertive; Conscientious; Apprehensive and Emotionally controlled. While the girls of both groups are possessing the personality factors as Reserve; Emotionally stable; Sober, Trusting; Tender-minded; Imaginative; Apprehensive; Dependent; Controlled and Relaxed.

CREATIVE POTENTIAL OF CONGENITALLY BLIND VISUALLY IMPAIRED (CB) AND ADVENTITIOUSLY BLIND (AB) CHILDREN

The Table 7.2 reveals that adventitiously blind children are having significant difference in relation to constituents of creative potential like-Flexibility and Originality.

The adventitiously group show the better development of flexibility and originality in comparison to the congenitally blind children. Analysis of data further show that both group are homogeneous on creative potential and its constituents i.e. Fluency.

GENDER-DISCRIMINATION AMONG THE VARIOUS GROUPS IN RELATION TO PERSONALITY FACTORS

The findings pertaining to gender discrimination are summarised in Table 7.3 The personality factors that significantly Ego-strength among the boys of all the groups (BB, NB, CBB and ABB). The girls of various groups are characterized by the qualities of Shyness; Conservatism and Group-dependence in their personality make up. BB Group believes in a fantasy life they are less practical and more dependent on their peers and family members. All the groups are appeared to be homogeneous on the factor-'B' which represent Poor intellectual development in them.

Table 7.3 : Gender Discrimination among the groups

Sl.	*PF Sym-bols*	*Personality Factor*	*BB BG* 1	*NB NG* 2	*CBB CBG* 3	*ABB ABG* 4	*Explanations*
1.	A	Reserved Vs Outgoing	*	*	*	*	The boys are extremely Superior in relation to the personality factor-A characterized by Affecothymia.
2.	B	Less Intelligence Vs More Intelligent	*	*	*	*	All the groups are appeared to be homogeneous except group 3 which represents

Sl.	*PF Sym-bols*	*Personality Factor*	*BB BG* 1	*NB NG* 2	*CBB CBG* 3	*ABB ABG* 4	*Explanations*
							less intelligent group of girls.
3.	C	Affected by Felling	*	*	*	*	Among all the groups boys have Emotionally stable better build of ego strength than girls.
4.	E	Humble Vs Assertive	-	-	*	*	CBG and ABG groups are more assertive than the boys.
5.	F	Sober Vs Happy-go-lucky	-	-	*	*	The girls in group no. 3 and 4 appeared Happy-go-lucky than their counterpart. The remaining groups are homogeneous and swinging between desurgency to surgency.
6.	G	Expedient Vs Conscientious	*	-	-	-	Blind group is having comparatively mild expedient trend while the remaining groups are similar and conscientious.
7.	H	Shy Vs Venturesome	*	*	*	*	Girls among the groups are characterized by

Sl.	*PF Symbols*	*Personality Factor*	*BBBG 1*	*NBNG 2*	*CBBCBG 3*	*ABBABG 4*	*Explanations*
							the quality of shyness but boys shown the average trend between shyness and venturesome.
8.	I	Tough minded Vs Tender minded	-	*	*	*	All groups have been qualified with the factor of tender mindedness but the boys in the groups 2, 3 and 4 exhibit it in outstanding manner.
9.	L	Trusting Vs Suspicious	-	-	*	*	All the groups are having trusting qualities but the groups CBB and ABB expressed high trustworthiness.
10.	M	Practical Vs Imaginative	*	-	*	*	All the groups of Blind i.e. 1,3 and 4 have highly imaginative boys than the girls.
11.	N	Forthright Vs Shrewd	*	-	*	-	The boys among all the groups have shown shrewdness in their personality makeup, whereas the groups 1 and 3 represent it

Sl.	*PF Sym-bols*	*Personality Factor*	*BB BG* 1	*NB NG* 2	*CBB CBG* 3	*ABB ABG* 4	*Explanations*
							remarkably in the boys.
12.	O	Placid Vs Apprehe-nsive	-	*	*	-	All the groups NB and CBG exhibit significant variation in relation to the personality factor.
13.	Q1	Conservative Vs Experimenting	*	-	*	*	All the groups represent average qualities of conservative Vs experimenting. All the girls in the groups 1,3 and 4 are significantly fluctuate towards extreme end to mark the trend of conservatism.
14.	Q2	Group dependent Vs Self Sufficient	*	-	*	*	All the girls in the groups 1,3, and 4 have revealed the trend of group-dependence in their personality makeup while the boys have equipped themselves with the judicious mixture of group-dependence and self-sufficiency.

Sl.	PF Symbols	Personality Factor	BB BG 1	NB NG 2	CBB CBG 3	ABB ABG 4	Explanations
15.	Q3	Undisciplined Self Conflict Vs Controlled	-	*	*	-	All the groups have been characterized with the quality of superior emotionality but normal girls are emerged as more socially precise.
16.	Q4	Relaxed Vs Tense	-	-	*	-	The group-3 have highly relaxed CB girls where the remaining groups have calibrated this factor on average level.

* P< .01

BB-Blind boys CBB-Congenitally Blind boys
BG-Blind girls CBG-Congenitally Blind girls
NB-Normal boys ABB-Adventitiously Blind boys
NG-Normal girls ABG-Adventitiously Blind girls

GENDER DISCRIMINATION AMONG THE VARIOUS GROUPS IN RELATION TO CREATIVE POTENTIAL

The findings in relation to the gender discrimination on the test of creativity has been summarised in the table 7.4. The creative potential and its components that significantly emerged (Fluency; Flexibility and Originality) among the boys of all the groups. It further confirms that boys of all the groups are having differences in relation to creative potential.

These findings show that boys have many facilities and opportunities to develop the creative potential but in case of girls. Education system, family as well as community etc. do not provide the favourable opportunities to the girls for their development of creative potential.

Table 7.4: Gender Discrimination Among the Groups on Creative Potential and its Constituents

Sl.	*Constituents of Creative Potential*	*BB BG* 1	*NB NG* 2	*CBB CBG* 3	*ABB ABG* 4	*Explanations*
1.	Fluency	*	*	*	*	All the boys are extremely superior in the groups in the groups 1,2,3 and 4 in relation to the Fluency constituents of creative potential.
2.	Flexibility	*	*	*	*	The boys in the groups 1, 2, 3 and 4 have high flexibility component of creative potential in comparison than the girls.
3.	Originality	*	*	*	*	The originality scores excel the boys in their creative potential among all the groups under consideration.
4.	Creativity	*	*	*	*	Thus the ongoing trend of excellence on all the three constituents of creative potential favours the boys to achieve them outstanding superiority on its global score. It reveals a systematic gender discrimination irrespective of impairment or non-impairment.

* $P < 0.05$

*BB = Blind boys	**CBB= Congenitally blind boys
BG=Blind girls	CBG=Congenitally blind girls
NB= Normal boys	ABB=Adventitious blind boys
NG=Normal girls	ABG= Adventitious blind girls

FINDINGS BASED ON COMPARATIVE PERSONALITY PROFILES

Comparative personality profiles are presented in chapter VI which indicate the submissive nature of blind children in comparison to normal children. The blind children are having some clinical qualities like Affectothymia; Dominance and better build of their Super-ego. Venturesome; Tender-mindedness; Shrewdness and marked by Tension. Further it can be said that blind and normal groups are similar in relation to the personality factors- C; L; Q1 and Q2. Both groups (blind and normal) are dominated by the personality factors of Happy-go-lucky; Imaginative; Apprehensive and Controlled emotionality.

On the other hand congenitally blind (CB) children exhibited imaginative and Apprehensive trends but the adventitiously blind (AB) children are characterised by the personality factors like- Out going: Assertive; Conscientious; Tender-minded; Shrewd and better build of Emotionality. The groups CB and AB are having normally developed Ego-strength and lead a normal life without showing timid behaviour.

Gender discrimination profiles show that boys of all the groups are Out going; Tender-minded; Superior Self-control; whereas girls of blind, NI, CB and AB group are emotionally Less-stable. All blind children have urgent need for love and affection. All the groups appeared to be homogeneous on the factor 'B' which represent poor intellectual development in them.

8

EDUCATIONAL IMPLICATION AND REMEDIAL PROGRAMME

A knowledge of personality and creative potential of blind children as drawn above can be used to advantage in the design of appropriate and effective educational programme. The following are some of the implications that emerge for teachers, parents, educational organizations, administrators, curriculum planners, guidance workers and counsellors, voluntary organisation and teacher-training institutions.

TEACHERS

Children are heavily influenced by people with whom they are in close personal contact. Teachers are like pillars that strengthen the educational structure and have many functions to perform within the class room and school atmosphere. A teacher of the blind should use the knowledge of the personality of these children in the teaching-learning process.

The teacher is in a position to facilitate the enrichment of the positive personality traits, and alleviate the effect of the negative ones through aids for discipline, communication, motivation and classroom organisation in the following manner:

1. Blind children respond favourably to kindness and sympathy in the teaching-learning atmosphere. The child may be motivated to behave with discipline

through such methods as rewards, grading, praise and encouragement by the teacher. These would also assist in the development of their emotional construction and good empathetic relationships.

2. Teaching in a friendly manner with due consideration to the problems of the students and appropriate new methods of teaching (through projects, comprehension, real-situation practicals etc.) which would promote their imagination, creativity, curiosity, interests, intellectual level and reduce negative attitudes such as aggression, tough-mindedness, anxiety, tension and dependency. A conducive and encouraging teaching-learning atmosphere would help in making the students realistic and sensual. Thus ameliorating their tendency to develop paranoid characteristics.
3. Reinforcing positive traits in the blind as well as normal children by teaching them it to communicate better through oral method audio tape and embossed material and braille content etc. Teachers should especially choose to teach interesting topics in order to develop the child emotionally and to involve them intellectually and help them to think imaginatively they should be urged to perform manual, creative and vocational tasks to make them explorative, creative and to put them in situations, where they are needed to interact amongst themselves.
4. Inclusion of co-curricular activities like-drama, music, playing the musical instrument, and sports as part of their subject. Mutual and inter- school competitions can be instituted and the children can be involved and motivated by announcement of their contribution in assembly.
5. Giving them an understanding of their own problem, helping them to develop a realistic perspective of themselves and the world around without either embarrassing or scaring them. Extensive use of audio

aids such as audio tape, talking book illustrate their impairment, their problems and way to conquer them aids like auditory instructions, audio tape, T.V. embossed globes, talking books, maps, pictures, clay model, discussion etc. should be used in every school for the blind to help them and to cope with the realities of the world with independent ideas.

PARENTS

The parents of the blind play a vital role in the emotional and intellectual development of these children. They must attempt to prevent feeling of inferiority among blind children by treating them as equal with the other siblings and normal children. On the other hand parent can promote these as normal children to co-operate with blind children. Since blind children are given to drawing in and becoming overly introspective, the parents can help by exposing them to social situations that encourage them to interact with others. The blind children have a tendency to be inhibited in their sexuality and have anxiety concerning their bodily functions, the family atmosphere play a major role in developing the sensuality and a respect for the body and its natural functions without being ashamed of the same. It is necessary for this that the blind child is not teased and made fun for its handicap.

They must therefore, be acquainted with the causes and problems of these isolated personality factors and lower creativity through media such as T.V. films, radio-talks, drama, parent-teachers associations and orientation programmes in schools and outside. This would help them to recognize traits which are to be encouraged and those to be rectified.

ADMINISTRATORS

Administrators should organize the school management in a manner that takes into account the personality structure especially of the blind and their problems and capabilities. They might help through making provisions to institutions the systems and the organisation. Such as time-table planning, curriculum design, co-curricular activities, creative activities, games and sports, and competitions etc., rather than leaving these components to the whims and initiative of the teachers. Therefore, the administrators could take measure such as improving class-room organisation by providing well- planned class-rooms to promote interaction. The seating plan should be such as to encourage individual participation. Good physical arrangements, availability of basic amenities, cleanliness, ventilation, play, stills board, embossed maps, globe, braille material, audio-tape etc. to enrich their personalities and creative abilities and provide a conducive atmosphere.

CURRICULUM PLANNERS

Blind children are found to be educationally backward as compared to normal due to their seemingly lower intellectual efficiency, weak emotional construction, low creative potential and ability to objectify their problems. New curricula suited to their personalties should be planned by incorporating large number of illustrations, rich braille literature, embossed model, practical knowledge manual and creative craft and vocational work. A suitable curriculum would make them more understanding, reasonable and well-adjusted to their personality characteristics. Special curricula can be useful in special schools, but in integrated systems they should be based on the mental efficiency of the individual child. Text books may contain standard subject matter, but with more illustrations.

TEACHER TRAINING INSTITUTIONS

Teachers should undergo in-service training demonstrations and social welfare institutions to get trained as resource teachers who strive to remove the negative personality trait, and promote positive traits alongwith the creative potential in the blind with a keen understanding of their problems, capacities, feeling and qualities. They can use the best available audio aids and new methods of teaching instead of sticking to traditional methods. These resource teachers can train their students to face life boldly in a society dominated by sighted individuals.

GUIDANCE WORKERS AND COUNSELLORS

Guidance plays an important role in changing the people's attitude and behaviour. Guidance workers and counsellors can arrange suitable counselling programmes related to academic matter or to solve their problems related to vision and vocational interest, and make them more intellectual, social, imaginative, practical, forth right, creative and emotionally balance. These guidance services should educate the parents and the public to be aware of the handicap, and help them to understand their isolated special personalities and attitudes, get trained in techniques and way of communication with the blind and most importantly develop a sympathetic attitude towards the handicapped.

EDUCATIONAL ORGANIZATIONS

Educational organizations such as UGC, NCERT, NIVH and NIEPA and educational planners should arrange orientation programmes to enrich the teachers with new innovative programmes, new curricula with pictorial illustrations, maps and practical exercises and comprehension questions with a work book as a supplement to the text book of each subject. This would facilitate a better understanding of the subject, help in the development of positive personality factors through making the students to feel competent and participative in the learning process. Since the blind children obtain from practical involvement, the teachers can incorporate new methodologies suited to their personalities with the use of oral practice, practical experimentation and audio films, audio tapes of lessons etc. to make education productive and self supportive. The blind students might be provided large variety of options such as vocational training, craft, carpentry candle making, canning, music, tailoring, weaving, etc. and other such vocations that involve little visual interaction.

VOLUNTARY ORGANISATION

Voluntary organizations bearing in mind the global personality structure of the blind children, can organize the vocational course, co-curricular activities, financial assistance, medical aid, free braille literature and lectures with the voluntary assistance of psychiatrists, doctors, educationists, psychologists and teachers. This would promote their welfare, encourage their balanced personality configuration and help them to become self-sufficient, vocationally trained, adjustable and independent individuals.

REMEDIAL PROGRAMME

On the basis of global personality makeup it can be analyzed that the blind group has some negative trends in their personality like Less intelligence, have Pessimistic behaviour more Imaginative and Less Sufficient or more dependent as given in Table 8.1.

Table 8.1: Negative Personality Trends Prevalent Among Blind Children

S.No.	*PFNo.*	*PF Symbol*	*Description of Personality Factors*
1.	2	B	Less intelligence
2.	5	F	Desurgency
3.	10	M	Careless
4.	14	Q2	Group dependent

To equip and compensate these personality factors the researcher has evolved out the following remedial programme.

1. Blind children are remarkably piled up in the lot of less intelligent children and suffered by the problem of poor achievement. This can be improved through proper education and training, and teaching programme heavily rely on auditory instruction,

memory based instruction, effective use of touch and senses, talking books, audio tapes, various programme should be used. The education programme should be launched in various area and provides the sizeable braille library in various languages and also subscribes to several braille magazines. The National Association for the Blind (NAB) encouraging the above education programme. Thus a blind person needs a little extra attention and care to help him to combat the hazards of blindness and learn to level the life of a normal person.

2. It is evident from the present study that blind children show the pessimistic behaviour or desurgency quality because blind children are found full of guilty complexes due to impairment of vision. School children needs to be help by their parents, peers and also some organizations, so they are encouraged to make good use of remaining senses. These children have to be encouraged to explore the house, the kitchen, the surrounding of house and neighbourhood in order to help them in attaining some degree of confidence. According to Blind Men Association (BMA) the education of blind is not enough, he has to be equipped with job oriented courses. Blind person are also capable in various career development courses such as Telephone operating. Stenographer; Salesmanship; Office management, Electrical course and Plumbing etc.

3. Visual impaired children show one more peculiar factor in their personality makeup that these children are careless about practical matters. Presence of this factor indicates that the blind children are unconcerned over everyday maters and this imagination leads to unrealistic situation accompanied by expressive outburst. To promote the attentiveness to practical matters of blind children. Schools are provided a

wealth of opportunities to take part in various co-curricular activities and competitions like Declamation contest, Poetry recitation, Essay writing and Group discussion etc. Such children need to be provided with rich stimulation and concrete experiences by taking them to field trips, picnics, excursions and recreational camps and sports meet. These activities help to the development of practice and conventional qualities of personality make- up of blind children.

4. Mostly blind children show the dependent personality trend. Such children to go along with the group and may be lacking in individual resolution. It is necessary to develop the confidence in their behaviour to develop the job oriented skills. These skill are suitable remuneration employment and self employment in the area of Tailoring, Canning, Weaving, Beg making, Book binding, Knitting, Motor and Armature winding, Carpentry etc. The Blind Boys Academy (BBA) at Narendrapur, West-Bengal started industrial vocational training. These efforts have led to employment of many blind persons. Employers and employing agencies should be encouraged through Government intervention to employ blind persons.

5. The special feature of the present study is that blind girls have a poor creative potential. Because the fate of blind woman is even more worse, birth of blind girls assumed to bring a life-long burden on the family. To improve the status of blind women, the school and training centres should be established exclusively for blind woman. The ideas of women's lib have recently caught fast in the SBWM's Woman Section. The society has established a woman committee. The committee has launched in vigorous programme of Cooking, Crafts, First aid, Knitting, Home decoration, Tailoring and even Dancing. Only one committee is not sufficient for the advancement of the status of blind women. So

more Committee, Woman's Section and Training centre should be needed to the development of creative potential.

SUGGESTIONS FOR FURTHER RESEARCH

1. Personality of blind and normal children can be studied in more detail by taking a large sample to draw more fruitful generalisations.
2. The methods used in teaching to these children in our country can be analysed and compared with teaching practices used in other countries, suggestions can be solicited and modification made in the existing methods prevalent in our country.
3. A study of rehabilitation programme, welfare programme can be undertaken in various Institutions, Organisation, Voluntary and Non-voluntary agencies.
4. A study of status of literate and illiterate blind women in India can be conducted.
5. Development of aids, braille literature and preparation of notation, codes and various educational programmes are suitable for Indian condition, can be undertaken.
6. To explore extensive Personality of the blind children some more specific reliable and valid measuring tools can be developed by the researchers.
7. A survey of Educational facilities and Rehabilitation can be carried our in perspective of U.P.
8. Studies pertaining to Technology advances and their impact in class-room teaching- learning procedure can be undertaken.
9. A study of the blind adults studying in professional and academic courses in various universities can be conducted.
10. Small projects can be conducted at postgraduate and

doctoral level in various educational institutions. Projects and Surveys concerning teaching methods in practices, curricula, methods of evaluation, and forming of new curricula suitable to their personalities can be floated.

9

VOCATIONAL OPPORTUNITY FOR BLINDS: THE INDIAN SCENARIO

It is a well known fact that in India alone, one third of the world's blind population resides making India's share of about 8-9 million people. Blindness has a definite and distinctive effect upon the development of the individual's personality because at least 75-80% of all impressions which is sighted person gets, are registered through the sense of sight. Thus blindness proves to be a severe handicap.

Blindness from birth, need not by itself cause serious development delays, yet we know that a large number of congenitally blind children do meet with grave difficulties that result finally in deviant personalities. These children suffer in a number of ways of which affectional deprivation becomes the most acute and all pervading. Affectional deprivation comprises of unsympathetic behaviour, less attention, insecurity and it leads to neuroticism, anxiety, maladjustment, aggression and a host of other problems. A blind person in India lives under a curse. He is a burden on his family and is either abandoned or allowed to waste away. A **report on Blindness in India in 1944, referred that the burden of blindness is not that you cannot see the light, the people, houses and landscapes around you, it is that you have nothing to do the fill the long, endless weary hours of darkness; you are nothing to**

do to fill the long, you are condemned to poverty and misery, and you cannot take part in the social life around you. Modern Welfare does away with all this. The blind person is, in reality extraordinarily normal. Given him a normal upbringing, give him his schooling, train him in a useful trade and provide conditions favourable to his work and he can and he does his work properly and becomes a useful citizen as any other person, and of course, the happiest man on the earth.

Work is the foundation of a vibrant society and the basis of a fulfilled life. That is why, the ancient Jewish sage firmly believed that the greatest help on individual can give another, is to provide him with work, to strengthen him until he no longer needs to ask for help. This holds true for every member of society, more so, far a disabled person. A job or self employment is not just an opportunity for a disabled individual, to contribute to society but also a means to change the way people perceive them.

A person, for no fault of his, acquires a disability at birth or at a later stage in his life, is put under a lot of pressure in all spheres of life. Unfortunately, unemployment is the biggest hurdle in the life of blind or infact, any disabled person. Apart from employment in formal sector, promotion of self-employment and Co-operative employment can help in providing viable income generation opportunities for disabled people. In many instance self-employment may be the only option as jobs are scarce in the open labour market and the blind person needs only vocational opportunity, not charity.

Realizing the need for on the job training for the disabled and their vocational orientation and training may organisation and institutes are taking up the challenge. The prominent organizations are:-

Blind Men's Association (BMA): It has started a multicategory workshop for handicapped children. BMA provides transitory training & employment, for various vocations and open placement opportunities. The National Association for the Blind (NAB) situated in Bombay imparts vocational training at various cities of Maharastra. The NAB provides training in the field of engineering, tailoring, assembling, fabrication of stationary items, carpentry, brush making and plastic molding. Infact, several trainees of NAB have found gainful employment in open industry.

Blind Relief Association (BRA): The another organisation in New Delhi, known as BRA has been running Industrial Home for the Blind. The sheltered workshop attached to this home gives training in handloom weaving and candle making.

The National Association for the Blind (NAB): This association has opened the doors of employment for the first time in India by employing blind people in textile mills. NAB Rehabilitation centre for the blind is one hand, providing the training in daily living skills like mobility, elementary braille, typing, home science etc. While on the other hand, NAB workshop for the blind provides the training in light engineering, carpentry, brush manufacturing tailoring, office files and plastic work. Several trainees of this workshop have been placed in remunerate employment. The Bureau of Self Employment of NAB provides financial assistance to assist the blind for starting a small business under the self employment scheme.

Tata Agricultural and Rural Training Centre for the Blind: It is located in Gujarat and engaged to provide the residential intensive training in the dairy and animal husbandry section. National Federation of the Blind is working to promote self help and self reliance among blind graduates. Today, it has several units in various parts of the country. Federation provides rehabilitation service, general education and vocational training to blind persons, the vocations taught include candle making, chalk making, plastic works, music, type writing.

National Institute of Visually Handicapped Children (NIVH): It is located Dehradun and provides transitory work experience and self employment opportunities to the blind people. NIVH has provision for skill development in agriculture, braille, bag scaling, binding, bag making, candle making, caning, detergent making engineering, knitting, music, office and management, sports, stenography, tailoring, typing, weaving etc. Psychological and Educational Test Unit helps to assess the abilities of the blind.

Blind Boys Academy (BBA): The BBA at Narendrapur. West Bengal had started Industrial Vocational Training. These efforts have led to gainful employment of many blind persons. Employers and employing agencies should be encouraged, through government intervention to employ blind persons.

Rajiv Gandhi Foundation: Recently the foundation has started to take keen interest in the job placement of disabled to generate confidence among them by encouraging financial independence. This is achieved by the National Center for the Employment of Disabled Persons (NCEDP). Which came to operation from August 1996. Their mission is to expand the activities at National level. It proposes to help the disabled to take their place as equal citizen of society. ACTIONAID is a British organization which supports Disability Rehabilitation is focusing for training of manpower in Rehabilitation centers to promote mobility and independence in disabled persons and also foster research into different aspects of rehabilitation. The Institute of Advanced Studies in Education of Rohilkhand University has also planned to start to Vocational Rehabilitation centre for disabled.

Another important point we want here is to discuss that vocational training to the disabled should be given after evaluating their attitude towards a particular trade or vocation. Training in modern technology should be imparted in sheltered workshops as well as in vocational training centers. Educational organizations such as UGC, NCERT, NIVH, NIEPA, AICTE and educational planners should arrange orientation programmes to enrich their curriculum and sources. The blind children might be provided large variety of options such as vocational training, craft, skill based programme, textile, computer, stenography, typing, office management and other such vocations that involve little visual interaction. This will promote their welfare, encourage them to become self sufficient, vocationally trained, adjustable and independent individuals.

BIBLIOGRAPHY

Abdi, V.& Zaidi, D.M. (1990): General Anxiety of visually handicapped children in relation to their grades, *Disability and Impairment*, 4(1)

Abraham, W. & Shankar, U. (1979): Educational for problem children. *Indian Psychological Review, 17(3)*

Ackoff, R.L. (1953): *The Design of Social Research*, University of Chicago Press, Chicago.

Advani, K.R. (1965): *Educational and Psychological Problem of the Blind Children in the age groups 7 to 21 years*, Ph.D., Bombay University, Bombay.

Advani, L.. (1981): A Comparative Study of Manneristic Behaviour of Blind and Sighted Children, *Research Monograph*, NIVH, Dehradun.

Advani, L. (1983): Technical Aids for the visually handicapped, *LBMRC Research News Letter*, 8(20).

Advani, L. (1983): Importance of Research in Rehabilitation *NASEOH News*, 15(2).

Agarwal, R. (1986): *A Study of Feeling of security in Morally developed and under-developed Adolescents as related to their Self-concept and Personality pattern*, Ph.D., Agra University, Agra.

Agarwal, R. (1992): Psycho social factors in mainstreaming Blind adults, *Journal of Visual Impairment & Blindness*, 86(2).

Agarwal, R.I., Singh, M.P. (1985): Role Imaginary and Non-frequency in paired Assorted Serial recall by the blind. *International Journal of Educational Sciences, (2)*

Agarwal, Y.P. (1988): *Better Sampling: Concepts Techniques and Evaluation*, Sterling Publishers Pvt.. Ltd. New Delhi.

Agrawal, Y.P. (1988): *Research in Emerging Fields of Education: Concepts Trends and Prospects*, Sterling Publisher Pvt. Ltd., New Delhi.

Allport, G.W. (1938): *Personality: A Psychological Interpretation*, Holt Reinhart & Winston Inc., New York.

Akkamadevi, B.A. (1984): *A study of the tactile discrimination ability of visually handicapped children and sighted children of Standard I-V*, M.Ed. Dissertation, Shri Ramkrishan Mission Vidyalaya College of Education, Coimbatore, Tamilnadu.

Anastasi, A and Schacfer, C. (1971): Notes on the concept of creativity and intelligence. *The Journal of Creative Behaviour*, 5(2).

Appelhans, P.(1993): Integration of Blind students, *European Journal of Special Needs in Education*, 8(3).

Ara, N.(1986): *Parents'personality, child-rearing attitudes and their children's personality An inter-correlation study*, Ph.D., Bhagalpur University, Bihar.

Arora, S. (1997) A programme for identifying visually Handicapped & Crippled Children, *Disabilities and Impairments*, Vol 11, No.2

Arora, S. (1998); Vocational apportunity for Blind, The Indian Scenario, *Disabilitis and Impairements*. Vol 12, No.1.

Arora, S. (1999):Personality configuration of Congenitally Blind children. *Social Science International*, Vol 15, No.2.

Arora, S. (2000): A study of creative Potential of congenitally visually impaired children, *Recent Researches in Education & Psychology*, Vol 5, No.2.

Arora, S. (2000): A comparative study of Creative potential of CB and AB children, *The Educational Review*, Vol 106, No. 7

Barbe, W.B. (1963): *An Exceptional Child,* Centre for Applied Research in Education Inc., New York.

Bagle, C. (1971): The Social psychology of the Child with Epilepsy, *Journal of Clinical Psychology,* 25(2), London.

Bala, M. (1986): A Comparative Study of the Mental make-up and Educational facilities for physically handicapped children, Ph.D. in *Buch's Third Survey of Research in Education,* NCERT.

Barbara, C.(1991): Families and Service in Autism, Promises to keep, *Dissertation Abstracts International,* 51(9)

Basu, A (1984): Teaching the Visually Handicapped: Research and Development Programme Needed, *NASEOH,* New York, 14(3)

Beaty, O.A. (1991): Psychological Adjustment and Academic achievement of visually handicapped University Students, *Dissertation Abstracts International,* 52(6).

Bhalerao, U. (1975): A Sociological Study of the Educated Blind in major urban centres of Madhya Pradesh, Ph.D. Thesis, Vikram University, Ujjain.

Bhalerao, U. (1983): *Educated Blind of Urban Madhya Pradesh,* Sterling Publication, New Delhi.

Bhan, R.N. (1975): Relationship between Creative Potential and the Level of Aspiration, *Journal of Education and Psychology,* 32(1)

Bhardwaj, R. (1997) Adequate depth of feeling and sex as correlates of the need for achievement among handicapped and non handicapped children . *Disabilities and Impairements* Vol.11.(2)

Bhatt, P. (1981): The Situation of Blind Woman in India, *Blind Welfare,* 23 (3)

Bhatia, P. (1993): Environmental Noise: An Impairing Agent, *Disabilities and Impairments,* 7(1), New Delhi.

Biglow, A.E. (1993): Locomotion and Search behaviour in blind infants. *Psychological Abstracts,* 80(1).

Binet, A. (1916): A History of the Care and Study of Exceptionals, Prentice Hall, New York.

Blackhurst, A.E. & William H.B. (1981): *An Introduction to Special Education,* Little Brown & Co., Boston.

Bonifacis, P. (1969): Creativity and the Projection of Movement Responses, *Journal of Projective Techniques and Assessment,* 33(4)

Brog, R. (1983): Educational Research: An Introduction, Longman, London.

Bose, S. and Biswa, C. 91972): A study of the Social World of Some Physically Handicapped Children, *Indian Journal of Applied Psychology, 9.*

Bose, S. and Banerjee, S.N. (1969): A resolution on the Personality Makerup of Some Institutional Physically Handicapped Children by the Children's Apperception Test, *Journal of Psychological Research,* 8(1).

Brambring, M. (1992): On the stability of Stereotyped Behaviour in blind infants and preschoolers. *Journal of Visual Impairment & Blindness,* 86(2).

Brown, P.A. (1938): Response of Blind and Seeing Adolescents to an Introversion Extroversion Questionnaire, *Journal of Psychology.*

Buch, M.B. (1974): Survey of Research in Education, *Centre of Advance Study in Education,* Baroda.

Buch, M.B. (1979): Second Survey of Research in Education, *National Council of Education Research and Training,* New Delhi.

Buch, M.B. (1983): *Third Survey of Research in Education,* National Council of Educational Research and Training, New Delhi.

Buch, M.B. (1988): *Fourth Survey of Research in Education,* 1 & II, NCERT, New Delhi.

Carrol, T.J. (1961): Blindness: What it is, what it does and how to live with it, Boston.

Cattell, R.N. (1946): *Description and Measurement of Personality*, N.W. World Book Co. Yonkes, New York.

Cattell, R.B. and Drevdahal, J.E. (1955): A Comparison of the Personality Profiles of eminent researchers with that of eminent teachers and administrators and of the general population. *British Journal of Psychology*.

Chatterji, P. S. (1983): *A comparative study of Personality, Intelligence and Achievement Motivation of Students in different Academic groups*, Ph.D., Patna University, Patna.

Chen, D. and Smith, J. (1992): Developing orientation and Mobility Skills in students who are Multi handicapped and Visually Impaired, *Rehabilitation and Education for Blindness and Visual Impairment*, Vol. 35(3).

Chattopadhyay, P.K. and Patil, A. (1982): Arousal in Handicapped Children: A study with blind subjects, *Child Psychiatry Quarterly*, 15(4).

Chua, T.T. (1993): Tertiary Education for Disabled Persons with emphasis on Visually Handicapped and Hearing-impaired individuals, *International Journal of Special Education*, 8(1)

Coleman, P.J. (1991): Exploring Visually handicapped children's understanding of length, *Dissertation Abstracts International*, 51(12).

Clair, D.N. (1989): Career Education competencies for elementary age students with visual impairment, *Dissertation Abstract International*, 50(5).

Crews, J.E. (1992): Measuring rehabilitation outcomes and the public policies on againg and blindness, *Journal of Gerontological Social Work*. 17(4).

Cutsforth, T.D. (1933): The blind in School and Society, *American Foundation for the Blind*, New York.

Dabhade, A (1985): Personality of Cross-Culture groups

studying in Dayalbagh Educational Institute, M.Ed. *Dissertation*, Dayalbagh Educational Institute, Agra.

Deasi, H.J.M. (1981): Rehabilitation of the blind in rural setting, *Social Welfare, 27(12).*

Deasi, H.J.M. (1982): Mobility Research Potential in Science & Technology in the Service of the blind, *LBMRC Research News Letter* 6(4).

Dellas, M. and Gair, E. (1970): Identification of Creativity: The *Individual Psychological Bulletin*, 73.

Dixit, A.K. (1985): Achievement in Education of Visually Impaired Children in India: A statistical Evaluation, *International Journal of Educational Science*, (2)

Date-Kwan, J. (1991): The relationship between early experience and development of young children with visual impairments. *Dissertation Abstracts International* 52, (3).

Dubey, P (1975): Intelligence and creativity and Rorschach in Indian Context, The Academic press, Gurgaon, Haryana.

Ezika, F. (1987): A comparative study of the development of self concept in normally sighted and blind students, *Dissertation Abstract International*, 48(2).

Frank, E, (1973): Is Creativity an Innovation in Education, *Education Trend, 8(4)* Ajmer.

Frank, Herbert G. (1993): Flash and Pattern-reversal visual evoked potential abnormalities in infants and children with cerebral blindness, *Psychological Abstract*, 80,(2).

Ghai and Sen (1985): Work Adjustment and Job Anxiety of the handicapped in open employment. An empirical study, *Indian Journal of Industrial Relation.*

Gilbertson, D.L. (1991): Explanatory style as a predictor of Psycho Social Adjustment among adventitiously blind adults, *Dissertation Abstracts International*, 52(6).

Goel, S.K. (1985): *Blindness and Visual Impairment*, Socio-Psychic Scientific Information Bureau, Delhi.

Goodman, I.F. (1992). Perceived need of high school teachers in public school setting where blind students are educated with their sighted classmates, *Dissertation Abstracts International,* 53,(5).

Government of United States Public Law, PL 94-142, (1975): *Education for all Handicapped Children's Act,* Government Printing Office, Washington, DC U.S.A.

Government of India, *National Policy on Education* (1986): Ministry of Human Resource Development, Department of Education, New Delhi.

Groenveld, M. and Jan, J.E. (1992): Intelligence profiles of low vision and blind children. Special Issue: Low vision, *Journal of visual Impairment and Blindness,* 86,(1).

Guilford, J.P. (1973): *Fundamental Statistics in Psychology and Education,* Mc.Grew Hill, New York.

Gupta, S.M. (194): A study of Demographic and Cognitive correlates of creativity. *Journal of Educational Research and Extension,* 30(4).

Haider, I. (1990): A comparative Study of some selected Psychological characteristic and Academic Achievement of Visually Handicapped children in special schools and in integrated setting, M.Ed. *Dissertation,* Jamia Millia Islamia, New Delhi.

Haider, S.I. (1982): The importance of teaching Science and Mathematics to the blind. *Blind Welfare* 24,(3).

Hallahan, O.P. & Kauffman, J.M. (1988): *Handbook Exceptional Children: Introduction to Special Education,* 4th Ed., International Inc; New York.

Hallahan, O.P.& Kauffman, J.M. (1988): *Handbook of Special Education,* Prentice Hall, Englewood Cliffs, New Jersey.

Handleman, P. (1990): The educational progress of normal peers in an integrated preschool class with autistic children, *Psychological Abstracts,* 78(5).

Hays, S.P. (1950): *Measuring the Intelligence of the Blind in Blindness*, Princeton, N.J. Princeton University Press.

Hech, A.O. (1953): *The Education of Exceptional Children*, Mc Grow Hill Book Company, Inc New York.

Hoffman, E. (1975): The American Public School and the deviant child: The origin of the involvement, *Journal of Special Education, 9(1).*

Indian Council of Medical Research (1975): *Co-ordinated Study of Prevalence of Blindness*, I.C.M.C., New Delhi.

Ityerah, M. and Gupta, V.R. (1981): A comparative study on congenitally blind and sighted on factual size, form perception and handedness, *Indian Journal of Public Administration.*

Jangira, N.K. Mukhopadhyay, S. and Rath, K.B. (1985): Survey of Research in Special Education in India, Department of Teacher Education, *Special Education and Extension services*, NCERT.

Joshi, P.L. and Bhattacharya, M. (1993): Handicapped persons; A demographic profile in a rural areas of U.P., *Disabilities and Impairments*, 2(2).

Kapoor, P. and Sen, A. (1989): *A Comparative Study of the Congenitally and Adventitiously blind with their Sighted Peers on Some Psychological Variables*, Atlantic Publisher and Distributor, New Delhi.

Kaul, G. (1985): A study of Attitude, reactions and awareness about Integrated Education of Visually Handicapped children, *Education*, 5.(1).

Kershaw, D.J. and Heinemann, W. (1961): *Handicapped Children*, Book Ltd. London.

Kirk, S.A. (1962): *Education Exceptional Children*, Oxford & IBH Publishing Co., Calcutta.

Kleinschmidt, J. (1992): The Psychological impact of visual impairment in older adults. *Dissertation Abstracts International*, 52(7).

Kool, V.K. (1981): Memory of Blind People, Project Report: Ministry of Social Welfare, Government of India, New Delhi.

Kool, V.K. & Kulshreshtha, S.P. (1986): *Visually Handicapped: Research in Indian Perspective*, Jugal Kisore & Co. Dehradun.

Kulshreshtha, S.P. (1950): *Recent Advances in Psychological and Educational Testing*, Jugal Kishore & Co., Dehradun.

Kumar, S. (1992): Socio-educational correlates of Creativity among Secondary School Students in Arunachal, *Indian Education Review*, 27(1), NCERT, Delhi.

Kundu, R. and Sanyal, N. (1985): Muscular Sensation of the Blind and sighted persons: A comparative study, *International Journal of Educational Sciences*, 2.

Kundu, S. (1968): Role of Physical Education in the Education of the Blind. *Journal of Psychology and Education* 3-(1).

Lal, A. (1992): *A study of the Personality, Mutual Perception Attitude and Vocational Preference of the Blind and the Sighted*, Ph.D. (Education), Allahabad University.

Lata, K (1985): The Impact of Parental Attitude on Social Emotional and Educational Adjustment of Normal and Handicapped Students in *Survey of Research in Education*, (1983-84), Vol. II, M.B. Buch, NCERT, New Delhi.

Latharam, J.K. (1983): Self-confidence and Self acceptance in blind and sighted adolescent boys, M.Ed. *Dissertation*, Department of Psychology, University of Madras.

Lowrence, B. (1991): Self-concept Formation and Physical handicap: Some educational implications for Integration. Disability, *Handicaps and Society*, 6(2), U.K.

Lowenfeld, V. (1950): Psychological Foundation of special methods in teaching blind children. *Blindness*, Princeton University Press.

Mackinnon, D.W. (1980): Research on creativity in creativity research, *International Perspective*, NCERT.

Mandal, B.B. (1975): Physically handicapped in Bihar in *Fourth Survey of Research in Education*, Vol. II, M.B.Buch, NCERT, New Delhi.

Mason, H.L. (1992): Use of the Blind Learning Aptitude Test with children in England and Wales and the United States. *Journal of Visual Impairment & Blindness*, 85(8).

Maxon, B.J. Tedder, S. and Lamb, A.M. (1993): The Education of youths who are Deaf Blind: Learning Tasks and Teaching Methods. *Journal of Visual Impairment and Blindness*, 87(7).

McAndrew, H. (148): Rigidity and Isolation: A study of deaf and blind, *Journal of Abnormal and Social Psychology*.

Mahadevan, K. (1993): Social Development, Cultural Change and Fertility Decline: Study in Kerala and Andhra Villages. *European Journal of Special Needs*, 8.(3) U.K.

Mehdi, B. (1976) *Verbal Test of Creative Thinking*, Agra National Psychological Corporation, Agra.

Minter, J. (1991): Recognition of Verbally Expressed Emotions by congenitally blind children, *Psychological Abstract*, 79(5)

Minter, M.E. and Pring (1992) Recognition of vocally expressed emotion by congenitally blind children. *Journal of Visual Impairment and Blindness*, 85(10).

Mittler, P. (1970): *The Psychological Assessment of Mental and Physical Handicapped*. Methuen & Co. Ltd., London.

Mishra, V.S.A. (1975): Socio-emotional factors determining Social Aggression among blind, M.A. (project Work), Agra University, Agra.

Mittal, A.K. (181): Research in the Education of the Blind, *Blind Welfare*, 23(2).

Mittal, A.K. (1984): Towards unfettered Employment Policy for the blind, *Braille International*, 6(3).

Mittal, S.R. (1985): A comparative study of blind and sighted Adolescents on some Personality Factors. *International Journal of Educational Science*, 2.

Nagpal, V. (1972): A Study of Adjustment Problems of the Blind, Dissertation submitted to Delhi University, Delhi.

Narayan, J.P. (1992): The effect of Modelling in teaching mentally retarded children, *Disabilities and Impairments*, 7(1).

National Sample Survey Organisation, Govt. of India (1981-83): Thirty Six Round, *Report of Survey of Disabled Persons*, 1981, Department of Statistics, New Delhi.

Nijhawan, R.C. (1983): Aggression in the blind. Blind Welfare, 25(2).

Njoroge, M.C.M. (1992): Factor Influencing Institution of Successful Mainstreaming of Visually Handicapped student in Kenya, *Dissertation Abstracts International*, 52 (12)

Pal, N. and Nigam, J. (2000): A comparative study of Adjustment of Blind students of General, SC and ST caste, '*Bhartiya Aadhunik Shiksha*, Vol 18. No.3.

Paige, K. (1989): The Unierant Model for Educating Visually Handicapped Children; Teacher Perception Role, Administrative Support, and Competencies Strunwaser, *Dissertation Abstract International*, 50(5).

Pal, S.K. and Saxena, P.C. (1985): Quality Control in Educational Research, Metropolitan Co., New Delhi.

Panda, F. (1985): A study of the job satisfaction of the teachers of Visually Handicapped Children, M.Ed. Dissertation, Shri *Ram Krishna Mission Vidyalaya, College of Education*, Tamil Nadu.

Pandey, R.N. (1985): A study of Affectional Deprivation, Ego-strength and Adjustment Pattern among Visually handicapped Children and their Rehabilitation in *Fourth Survey in Education*, Vol. 11, M.Buch (1983-88), NCERT, New Delhi.

Pathak, A.B. (1984): A study of Disabled children in normal schools in *Fourth Survey of research in Education*, Vol. 11, M.B. Buch, (1983-88), NCERT, New Delhi.

Pathak, K.C. (1985): Socio-Psychological Problems of Visually Handicapped Children, *Blind Welfare* 276,(3).

Pathak, K.C. and Bahuguna, S.P. (1985): Socio-Psychological problems of the Rural Blind Child, *LBMRC Research News Ltter,* 9,(4).

Petric H. and Gill, J. (1993): Short Report: Current research on access to graphical user interfaces for visually disabled computer users, *European Journal of Special Needs Education,* 8, (2).

Premavathy, V. and Devappu, S. (1992): Effectiveness of using adopted geometrical aids for learning geometry by visually handicapped children, Research Highlights, *Journal of Avinashilingam Institute for Home Science & Higher Education for Women,* Deemed University, Coimbatore, 2(2).

Poplowski, R.K. (1992): Prevalence and Psycho social factors influencing Depression among adult blind residents of Utah, *Dissertation Abstract International, Vol. 52,* No. 12.

Public Law 94-142: The Education of All Handicapped Children Act, November, 1975.

Punani, B. (1997): Comparative evaluations of the effectiveness of various modes of education of blind children. *Disability and Impairment,* Vol 11(2).

Qadri, A. and Hussain (1985): Certain Social Psychological dimensions among handicapped and non-handicapped students, *Perspective in Psychological Researches,* 5.

Rai, P (1988): *A Comparative Study of Personality Dynamics of Blind and Sighted Higher Secondary Students,* Ph.D., Gorakhpur University, Gorakhpur.

Rangaswami, K.(1985): Hysterical blindness in childhood, *Child Psychiatry Quarterly,* 18,(1).

Ray Chaudhry, M. (1962): Creativity and Personality, *Journal of General Psychology,* 69.

Reddy, S.N. (1996) Personalities correlates of coping behaviour in the physically handicapped students. *Disabilities and Impairments,* Vol 11 (1).

Reddy, G.L. Rajaguru (1998), A study of Divergent thinking, convergent thinking and Mental ability of congenital blind children in secondary schools. *Disability and Impairments,* Vol 12, No. 1.

Rees, M.E. and Goodman, M. (1961): Some relationship between Creativity and Personality, *Journal of General Psychology,* 65.

Richards, A.S. and Muni, M. (1991): Computer Technology and Exceptional Individuals, Media and Technology for Human Resources Development, 3.

Sahoo, J. (1991): A comparative study of the behavioural characteristics of the Blind, Deaf, Dumb and Normal children of Orissa, M. Phil. Diss., Ravenshaw College, Cuttack.

Sangeeta (1996): A comparative study of the learning aptitudes of the congenitally and adventitiously blind pupils. *Disability and Impairment. Vol.* 10(02).

Sen, A. (1988): *Psychological Integration of the Handicapped: A Challenge to the Society,* Mittal Publications, New Delhi.

Sengupta, P.C. (1993): Factors of Education and Blind Child, 13th Birthday Dr. Helen Killer, New Delhi.

Serpell, R. (1992): The development of a community based strategy for the rehabilitation of disabled children in Zambia: A case of Action Oriented Health Systems Research, *Disabilities and Impairments,* 2(2).

Sharma, M.S. (1969): *Comparative Study of the Personality Adjustment of the blind and Sighted,* Ph.D. Thesis, Gujarat University, Ahmedabad.

Sharan, G. (1979): *Originality and Fluency in relation to Academic Achievement at High School Level,* Ph.D. Thesis, Rohilkhand University, Bareilly.

Shawn, D.G. 91993): Educational provisions for children with

Disabilities, Parents' opinions and general conclusions, *Disabilities and Impairments*, 4(2) & 5(2).

Singh, R.P. and Prabha, S. (1987): Evaluation of Integrated Educational Facilities for Physically Handicapped in the Schools of Bihar in *Fourth Survey of Research in Education*, (1983-88(M.B. Buch, 2, NCERT, New Delhi.

Singh, R.M. and Neilsworth, J.T. (1975): *The Exceptional child: A functional Approach*, McGraw Hill Inc., New York

Singh, T.B. (1984): Experiences in a pshychological clinic for the visually handicapped papers presented at 15th Annual Conference of Indian Association of Clinical Psychologists.

Singh, T.B. and Bhandari, K. (1984): Personality Assessment of Visually handicapped on Hindi E.P.Q. Paper presented at the 15th Annual Conference of India Association of Clinical Psychologists, (December 28-30th), Dehradun.

Singh, T.B. and Pathak, K.C. (1984): A personality study of visually Handicapped Persons, *LBMRC Research News Letter*, 9, (1).

Singh, D.P. (1976): A comparative study of the effectiveness of Programme Learning material in the achievement of blind and sighted children in modern mathematics taught by different methods, Ph.D. Thesis, Delhi.

Sommers, V.S. (1944); The influence of Parental Attitudes and Social environment in the Personality development of adolescent blind, American Foundation for the Blind, New York.

Telford, C.W. and Sawrey, M. (1977): *The Exceptional Individual*, Prentice Hall International, Inc, London.

Thronton, E. and Guilford, J.P. (1972): Creativity: Retrospect and Prospect, *The Journal of creative Behaviour*, 5

Troster, H. and Brambring, M. (1993): Early Social Emotional Development in Blind Infants, *Pshychological Abstract*, 80,(1)

Verma, J. (1990): *Creativity and Research in Indian Context*, Academic Press, Gurgaon.

Verret, A.D. (1992): Community adjustment and vocational stability of graduates of a state residential school for students with visual impairment, *Dissertation International,* 53(5).

Vyas, R.T. (1958): *Visually handicapped in the Bombay, their Social Background and Present Status*, Ph.D. Thesis, Bombay University, Bombay.

Walffe, K.E. and Schriner, K.F. (1992): Employment concerns of people with blindness or visual impairment, *Journal of Visual Impairment & Blindness,* 86,(4).

Wall, W.D. (1979): Constructive Education for Special Groups: Handicapped and Deviant Children, George G. Garrap & Co. Ltd., London.

Warnock, M. (1979): Special Educational Needs: A brief guide to the report of the Committee of Enquiry in the Education of Handicapped children and Young People, London.

Williams, K.E. (1986): A study of Adjustment of the blind and deaf students in standard V, VI & VII of special schools in Karnataka, Horizen College of Education, Bangalore, In *third Survey of Research in Education,* M.B.Buch, NCERT, New Delhi.

Woo, I. (1991): Blind students, Perception and Interaction with moving objects, *Dissertation Abstract International,* 55 (6).

APPENDIX - 1

General Information Questionnaire (GIQ)

1. Name : ....
2. Sex (Male/ Female): ....
3. Class: ....
4. Section : ....
5. School Name : ....
6. Date of Birth : ....
7. Age : ....
8. Handicapness before birth or : ....
   after birth
9. Cast : ....
10. Religion : ....
11. Citizenship : ....
12. Name of the State which you are : ....
    residing
13. City/ Village/ Block : ....
14. Residence area (Rural/ Urban) : ....
15. You are hostler/ day scholar : ....
16. Birth sequence

Family Information

1. Father's Name : ....
2. Education of Father : ....
3. Occupation : ....
4. Income of Father : ....
5. Mother's Education : ....
6. Mother's occupation : ....
7. Income of mother : ....
8. Any other source of income : ....
9. Total income of family : ....
10. Total no. of sibling : ....
11. Impairdness of any other family : .... member

School Information

1. Percentage of marks of last class : ....
2. Do you like your subjects : ....
3. Do you get vocational education : ....
4. Facilities in class room

   a. Good ....   b. Satisfactory ....

   c. Not satisfactory ....
5. Facility of library

   a. Satisfactory   b. Not satisfactory
6. In your library no. of books are sufficient (Yes / No)
7. Your school has play ground : (Yes / No)
8. You have reader facility : (Yes / No)
9. You get scholarship : (Yes / No)
10. You likes your friends : (Yes / No)

APPENDIX - 2

Form-D

What to do: Inside this booklet are some question to see what attitudes and interests you have there are no "right" and "wrong" answers because every one has the right to his own views. To be able to get the best advice from your results, you will want to answer them exactly and truly.

If a separate "answer sheet" has not been able given to you, turn this booklet over and tear off the answer sheet on the beak page.

Write your name and all other information asked for on the top line of the answer sheet.

First you should answer the four sample question below so that you can see whether you need to ask anything before starting. Although you are to read the question in this booklet you must record your answers on the answer sheet (alongside the same number as in the booklet).

There are three possible answers to each question. Read the following examples and makr your answers at the top of your answer sheet where it says "Example." Fill in the left-hand box if your answer choice is the "a" answer, in the middle box if your answer choice is the "b" answer, and in the right – hand box if you choose the "c" answer.

Example

1. I like to watch team games.

   a. yes, b. occasionally, c. no.

2. I prefer people who:

   a. are reserved,

   b. (are) in between,

   c. make friends quickly.

3. Money cannot bring happiness.

   a. yes (true), b. in between, c. no (false).

4. Woman is to child as cat is to:

   a. kitten, b. dog, c. boy.

In the last example there is a right answer-kitten. But there are very few such reasoning items.

Ask now if anything is not clear. The examiner will tell you in a moment to turn the page and start. When you answer, keep these four points in mind.

1. You are asked not to spend time pondering. **Give the first, natural answer as it comes to you.** Of course, the questions are too short to give you all the particulars you would sometimes like to Have. For instance, the above question asks you about "team games" and you might be fonder of football than basket ball. But you are to reply "for the average game," or to strike an average in situations of the kind stated. Give the best answer you can at a rate not slower than five or six a minute. You should finish in a little more then half an hour.
2. Try **not** to fall back on the middle, "uncertain" answers except when the answer at either end is really **Impossible** for you-perhaps once every four or five questions.

3. Be sure not skip anything, **but answer every question, somehow**. Some may not apply to you very well, but give your best gueses. Some may seem personal; but remember that the answer sheets are kept confidential and cannot be scored without a special stencil key. Answers to particular questions are not inspected.
4. Answer as honestly as possible what is true of you. Do not merely mark what seems "the right thing to say" to impress the examiner.

1. I think my memory is better than it ever was.

   a. yes, b. in between, c. no.

2. I can easily go a whole morning without wanting to speak to anyone.

   a. often, b. sometimes, c. never.

3. If I say that water is "dry" and the sun is "cold," I would say that "found" means the same as:

   a. gone, b. lost, c. unknown.

4. I generally go to bed at night feeling that I've had a satisfying day.

   a. true, b. in between, c. false.

5. If I had plenty of money, I would:

   a. be careful not to make other people envious,

   a. uncertain,

   b. show people how to live well.

6. The worst punishment for me would be:

   a. hard labour,

   b. uncertain,

   c. to be shut up alone.

7. If my income were more than enough for ordinary daily needs. I would feel I should give the rest to a church or other worth while cause.

   a. yes, b. in between, c. no.

8. I'm the one who takes the first step in making new friendships.

   a. usually, b. sometimes, c. never.

9. On a free evening, I would prefer to read about:

   a. how to talk to people from abroad,

   b. uncertain,

   c. military defence against the enemy.

10. Most people "go lazy" on a job if they can get away with it.

    a. yes, b. uncertain, c. no.

11. When I was a child, I more often spent free time:

    a. building something,

    b. in between,

    c. reading.

12. I am much more fortunate than most people in being able to do thing I like.

    a. yes, b. uncertain, c. no.

13. I can always forget trivial, unimportant things that I have done wrong.

    a. yes, b. in between, c. no.

14. I I had a log of money to give tto charity, I would give it:

    a. all to scientific research,

b. half to each,

c. all to churches.

15. A seaside beach would be more appealing to me if there were:

    a. no people around,

    b. in between,

    c. lots of families at play.

16. If I were to mix alcoholic drinks at party, I'd probably:

    a. try to make them exactly as people want them,

    b. uncertain,

    c. surprising people by making them strong.

17. I offen jumpo to conclusion.

    a. yes, b. in between, c. no.

18. I have sometimes, even in briefly, had hateful feelings toward my parents.

    a. yes, b. in between, c. no.

19. I would prefer to be:

    a. business executive who attends one meeting after another,

    b. uncertain

    c. a research scientist.

20. I think the opposite of "right" is the opposite of:

    a. left b. wrong c. correct.

21. I feel that my emotions are:

    a. well satisfied

b. only partly satisfied

c. very little satisfied.

22. I admire more the person, who, when asked his opinion:

    a. wants to be sure of the details before deciding,

    b. in between,

    c. speaks right up, and shows where he stands.

23. I love to make people laugh with funny stories

    a. yes, b. in between, c. no.

24. I think most people take life:

    a. too seriously,

    b. in between,

    c. not seriously enough.

25. During an interview, whether it's important or not, I:

    a. feel "on edge" and ill at ease,

    b. between,

    c. feel confident and composed.

26. My friends are more likely:

    a. to ask me for advice,

    b. in between,

    c. to give me advice.

27. I think most people take their duties to the community seriously enough.

    a. true, b. in between, c. false.

28. There are some areas of knowledge that are better left alone.

    a. true, b. in between, c. false.

29. If I feel like telling someone just what I think of him, I:
    a. go right ahead and speak the truth,
    b. in between,
    c. first consider the consequences of my doing so.

30. I have more ups and downs in mood than most people I know.

    a. yes, b. in between, c. false.

31. Today we need more logical, cool thinking in social matters and less attachments to older ideas and loyalties.

    a. true, b. in between, c. false.

32. I prefer to eat lunch:
    a. with lots of other people,
    b. in between,
    c. by myself.

33. I'm careful and practical about things so that I have fewer accidents than most people.

    a. true, b. in between, c. false.

34. When something unexpected happens, I:
    a. Remain very composed or calm
    b. in between,
    c. become extremely nervous or tense.

35. It's hard for me to admit it when I'm wrong.

    a. true, b. in between, c. false.

36. As a hobby I would prefer to:
    a. build things,
    b. uncertain,

c. act in plays.

37. Which word does not belong with the other two?

a. by, b. after, c. near.

38. I have some special fears, for example, of certain animals, or being shut in, or crossings wide streets, or being along in the dark, and so on.

a. yes, b. in between, c. no.

39. I really can't blame people for trying to grab what they can.

a. true, b. in between, c. false.

40. If I had to choose one, I'd prefer a vacation which was:

a. relaxing,

b. I between,

c. filled with activities.

41. I value good manners and respect for rules more than easy living.

a. true, b. in between, c. false.

42. When I'm in a group of strangers, I'm usually one of the last to express my opinion publicly.

a. yes, b. in between, c. no.

43. I enjoy learning to work new gadgets in every day things, from can openers to cars.

a. yes, b. in between, c. no.

44. When people secretly say bad things about me, I:

a. forget it,

b. in between,

c. try to catch them at it.

45. In intellectual interests, my parents are (were):

    a. above average,

    b. average,

    c. a bit below average.

46. Many popular magazines are concerned with writing what most people want to read rather than with the truth.

    a. yes, b. in between, c. no.

47. I never let myself get depressed over trifles.

    a. true, b. in between, c. false.

48. I dislike seeing religious authority overturned by so-called progress and logical reasoning.

    a. true, b. in between, c. false.

49. There are times, every day, when I want to enjoy my own thoughts, uninterrupted by other people.

    a. yes, b. in between, c. no.

50. Many people believe my views on politic and society to be:

    a. very sound,

    b. in between,

    c. a little odd or unusual.

51. When I'm talking to people, outiside noises, passerby, etc., don't draw. My attention away from what I'm doing.

    a. true, b. in between, c. false.

52. When I know I'm doing the right things, I find my task easy.

    a. always, b. sometimes, c. seldom.

53. I'd prefer a job which requires lots of decisions in dealing with people.

    a. true, b. uncertain, c. false.

54. "Hot" is to "warm" as "mountain" is to.

    a. slope, b. plain, c. hill.

55. I get over disappointments:

    a. quickly, b. in between, c. slowly.

56. If I don't get my way with a clerk in a large company, I don't hesitate to go to her superior.

    a. true, b. in between, c. false.

57. I take it on myself to liven up a dull party.

    a. often, b. sometimes, c. never.

58. When I need immediately the use of something belonging to a friend but he's out, I think it's all right to borrow it without his permission.

    a. yes, b. in between, c. no.

59. I can easily start to talk with a group of strangers in a bus or waiting room.

    a. yes, b. in between, c. no.

60. As a job, I would prefer:

    a. writing or editing children's books,

    b. uncertain,

    c. repairing electrical machines.

61. Even in an important game, I am more concerned with enjoying it than with who wins.

    a. always, b. generally, c. occasionally.

62. I would rather think about my ideas than take part in athletic games.

    a. yes, b. in between, c. no.

63. I think it is wiser to keep the nation's military forces strong than just to depend on international goodwill.

    a. yes, b. in between, c. no.

64. I'm more easily upset by bad news than most people I know

    a. true, b. uncertain, c. false.

65. When I'm with a group of people, I agree with their ideas so that no arguments will arise.

    a. usually, b. in between, c. often disagree.

66. I would rather spend a free evening:

    a. with a good book,

    b. uncertain,

    c. working on a hobby with friend.

67. I like to find excuses to put off work and have fun instead.

    a. often, b. sometimes, c. rarely.

68. When I'm criticized, it disturbs me badly.

    a. yes, b. in between, c. no.

69. My mind doesn't work so clearly at some times as it does at others.

    a. true, b. in between, c. false.

70. I talk to people:

    a. to make them feel comfortable,

    b. in between,

    c. only when I have something to say.

71. I think the proper number to carry on the series 1, 3, 2, 4, 3, 5, is:

    a. 4, b. 6, c. 8.

72. I have the feeling that my blood pressure goes up very quickly when someone annoys me.

    a. yes, b. in between, c. no.

73. If I had to tell a person a deliberate lie, I'd have to look away, being ashamed to look him in the eyes.

    a. true, b. uncertain, c. false.

74. I would rate myself as a relatively casual and lighthearted person.

    a. yes, b. in between, c. no.

75. The sight of littered, untidy streets make me cross.

    a. true, b. in between, c. false.

76. I would like a job where I:

    a. have a lot of responsibility and can show my competence,

    b. in between,

    c. would be given definite tasks so that I always know what I'm supposed to do.

77. I would prefer to have:

    a. more money,

    b. uncertain,

    c. more time for thinking about life.

78. I any one betrays my trust, I:

    a. get very angry with him,

    b. in between,

c. soon forgive.

79. newspaper accounts of everyday dangers and accidents:
    a. make rather dull, trivial reading,
    b. in between,
    c. hold my attention.

80. I can do hard physical work without feeling worn out as quickly as most people do.

    a. yes, b. sometimes, c. no.

81. I don't feel guilty if I'm scolded for something I did not do.

    a. true, b. uncertain, c. false.

82. I would rather be known for:
    a. relying or depending on well-tried methods,
    b. in between,
    c. always trying new ideas.

83. I like to keep track, at least roughly, of where money is spent.

    a. yes, b. sometimes, c. no.

84. When I have to face a hard day of work, I:
    a. wish it would never come,
    b. in between,
    c. look on it as a challenge.

85. If I can't seem to solve a problem, I:
    a. try harder,
    b. in between,
    c. feel the problem is too hard for me.

86. I may be less considerate of other people than they are of me.

a. true, b. sometimes, c. false.

87. In my spare time I would rather join:

a. a hiking and exploring club,

b. uncertain,

c. a community service organisation.

88. I have pots numbered 1, 2, 3, and 4. Each holds twice as much as the next lower number. After I pour from a full 4 in to an empty 3, how many half-full I's can I still fill from 4?

a. 2, b. 4, c. 8.

89. When I get up in the morning, I feel I can hardly face the day.

a. often, sometimes, c. never.

90. If we are lost in a city and my companions disagree with me on the best way, I:

a. happily,

b. in between,

c. make no fuss, and follow them.

91. I would rather listen to music:

a. one at home,

b. uncertain,

c. with an audience in a large auditorium.

92. When I'm in bed with the flu or a bad cold:

a. I enjoy it as a sort of vacation,

b. Uncertain,

c. I feel worried and concerned about not working.

93. I feel I would have a great deal of difficulty giving a speech before an audience of strangers.

    a. true, b. uncertain, c. false.

94. Some of the things I enjoy involve the thrill of danger.

    a. yes, b. in between, c. no.

95. Most people get too upset over things of no importance.

    a. true b. uncertain, c. false.

96. I'd prefer:

    a. to go camping,

    b. in between,

    c. in attend an outdoor musical performance.

97. When I have to tell a friend something he won't like, I:

    a. get it done at the first opportunity,

    b. in between,

    c. put it off as long as possible.

98. I sometimes feel sorry for all the people in the world.

    a. yes, b. in between, c. no.

99. I most enjoy a meal if it consists of:

    a. usual, exotic foods,

    b. uncertain,

    c. standard, regular foods.

100. I enjoy being considered part of the group when my neighbours do anything.

    a. true, b. in between, c. false.

101. At times I feel smashing things.

a. true, b. in between, c. false.

102. Before a test or examination, I:

a. get tense and wrapped up in what's coming,

b. in between,

c. keep quite calm.

103. I may deceive people by being friendly when I really dislike them.

a. yes, b. sometimes, c. no.

104. Which word doesn't belong with the other two?

a. lead, b. win, c. succeed.

105. If Susan's mother's sister is Judy's great aunt, what relation is Judy's great aunt to Susan.

a. grandma, b. aunt, c. mother.

APPENDIX - 3

TCW
Dr. Bacqer Mehndi
Prof. of Education
NCERT
New Delhi - 110006

Name : .... Age : ....

Class : .... School Name : ....

Fathers Name : .... Occupation : ....

Address : .... Date : ....

Instruction

1. Novelty, originality and creative ability play an important role in man's life. All inventions are the result of man/s ability to think in novel ways. There are many things in this world which can be made more interesting and useful by the use of our imagination and creative thinking. People who possess this ability have been responsible for many new inventions and discoveries.

2. "On the following pages in this booklet you will find mentioned some interesting problems which, if tackled imaginatively and creatively, may result in interesting and novel responses. You will enjoy doing these problems.

3. "The activities given in this booklet relate to problems of your daily life. They do not have right or wrong answers. You have to think of as many novel and interesting things about them as you can. Try to think of such things as no one else in your class may have thought of. If fact, your novel and creative responses will enable us to know about your ability to think about things in a creative manner. Therefore, write as many novel and interesting ideas as you possibly can, even if they appear to you to be impossible.

4. "You have been given four activities to do. For convenience sake, each activity has been separately timed. Try to work as quickly as you can. If you finish an activity before the time for it is up, do not go to the next activity until you are told to do so. Use your remaining time to think quietly about the different tasks of the activity, and write whatever new ideas come to your mind about any of the task in that activity. At the end, you will be given five minutes extra. If you get any new idea about any of the problems which you could not mention at the time you were working on them, please write it in the extra time allowed to you.

5. "Attempt every task of the four activities. When you are asked to begin, immediately start your work. If you have to ask any thing, please do it now. If you have no difficulty now, but find one later, quietly raise your hand from your seat so that your difficulty may be removed".

Instructions

Activity I

1. On the following pages you have been given some situations which will appear to you as impossible. You have to think what would happen if such situations actually arise.

2. "Give as many ideas as may come to your mind but try to think as many novel ideas as you possibly can, ideas which you think no one else might have thought. Write your responses in the space provided.

3. "You will be given 15 minutes for the three items of this activity. After every five minutes you will be told the time so that you may move on to the next item in the activity.

4. "Below is given an example which will help you to know what you have to do.

Example : What will happen if birds and animals start speaking like man ?

Some possible responses:

i. This world will change into a different kind of society.

ii. New leaders will emerge from amongst the animals.

iii. It is possible that a donkey will become our Prime Minister.

iv. Men may confide their secrets to their animal friends."

Problems

a. What would happen if man start flying like birds ?

b. What would happen if our schools had wheels ?

c. What would happen if man does not have any need for food?

Instruction

Activity II

1. "On the following pages you have been names of certain things which could be used in many different and new ways. You have to think in how many different and new ways the things may be used.

2. "Write as many uses as you can, but try to think those

which are novel i.e. those which you think no one else might have thought.

3. "You will be given 12 minutes for the three items of this activity. After every four minutes you will be told the time so that you may move on to the next item in the activity.

4. "Below is given an example which will help you to know what you have to do.

Example : Newspaper.

Some possible responses :

i. To read the news

ii. To make paper toys.

iii. To get protection from sun.

iv. To wrap something

v. To cover a dirty place

   a. A piece of stone

   b. A wooden stick

   c. Use of water

Instruction

Activity III

1. "On the following pages you have been given pairs of words which can be related to each other in many different ways. You have to think in how many different and new ways are they related.

2. "Write as many relationship as you can, but also try to think those which are novel, that is, those which you think no one else might have thought.

3. You will be given 15 minutes for the three items of this activity. After every 5 minutes you will be told the time so that you may move on to the next item in the activity.

4. Below is given an example which will help you to know what you have to do.

Example : Man and Animal.

Some Possible relationships :

i. Both have life

ii. Both need food and water

iii. Both can fall it

iv. Both are afraid of enemy

v. Both have the experience of feeling cold and hot.

   a. Tree and House

   b. Chair and ladder

   c. Air and water

Instruction

Activity IV

"Just keep in mind a simple model of a toy horse. You have to imagine in what ways you can change this into an interesting and novel one. You may think of adding any number of parts or accessories in order to make it really beautiful and / or useful. Do not bother about the cost of the new parts or accessories that you would like to use.

"Write all the ideas that come to your mind in serial order in the space given below".

"You will be given 6 minutes for this activity".

When the time for Activity IV is up, the test-administrator should announce that 5 minutes extra time will be allowed so that anyone who wants to do additional work at any item may now do so.

INDEX

❑❑❑